LIBYA
THE HISTORY OF
GADDAFI'S
PARIAH STATE

LIBYA
THE HISTORY OF GADDAFI'S
PARIAH STATE

JOHN OAKES

The
History
Press

To June, Nikki and Becky

First published 2011

The History Press
The Mill, Brimscombe Port
Stroud, Gloucestershire, GL5 2QG
www.thehistorypress.co.uk

British Library Cataloguing in Publication Data.
A catalogue record for this book is available from the British Library.

ISBN 978 0 7524 6412 1

Typesetting and origination by The History Press
Printed in Great Britain
Manufacturing managed by Jellyfish Print Solutions Ltd

Contents

Acknowledgements

The kindness shown to my wife, June, our daughter, Nikki, and to me during eight and a half years of living and working in Libya needs more than mere acknowledgement. Whilst there June and I worked for, and with, many Libyans. We grew to respect and like them in equal measure. If justice is done they should all have had fine careers and now be retired with honour amongst their progeny.

Whatever merit there may be in this small book is due to others – in particular the two great anthropologists Professors E.E. Evans-Pritchard and Emrys Peters. Had he lived, I hope that Emrys Peters would have forgiven me where paraphrasing of his work has slipped into plagiarism. He set a standard that we who follow are unlikely to match. John Wright has written the best history of Libya and I recommend his work to all. There are many others of course, but they do not match these three greats.

Amongst the many in The History Press to whom I owe thanks, I would single out Chrissy McMorris who has found herself editing my work. I fear that I needed more editing than most and I am fortunate that she is both talented and decisive. Simon Hamlet had the courage to commission this small book and Gary Chapman the creative energy to give it life. I also thank Lindsey Smith and Abbie Wood.

My thanks go to the photographer, Tom Atkins, sometime of the Royal Army Veterinary Corps, whose images of Libya were fortunately collected by his colleague Peter Cox. I also thank Maureen Norgate for images of Tobruk and Cyrene. That of the King's Palace is rare indeed.

The errors of fact and syntax that remain despite the efforts of Chrissy McMorris and June Oakes are mine alone. I have done my best to find and acknowledge the copyright of words and images used in this book. If I have missed someone I would be happy to hear from them.

John Oakes
Libyastories.com

Author's Note

There are at least thirty-two ways of spelling Muammar Gaddafi in English and all of them are correct. I have chosen the spelling used by the BBC in 2011. There are also various ways of spelling other Arabic names in English. I have chosen the easiest versions and attempted to be as consistent as possible, not always successfully.

I often stopped for a rest, a coffee and hard-boiled egg in Ajadabia. I note that it is now called Ajdabia. Perhaps the reader will excuse my sentimental attachment to the old version and bear with me when we differ about the spelling of other names – Benghazi and Banghazi, Senussi and Senusi, for example.

Introduction

This is a small book about Libya written by an ex-Royal Air Force officer who served in that country for more than eight years. Its purpose is to tell you some of the reasons why Muammar Gaddafi came to power, stayed in power and used it controversially. It briefly examines the conditions in which he was born and the influences that shaped him.

It also attempts to illuminate the historical reasons for the differences between West, East and South Libya, which make the task of governing it so challenging.

When Libya gained independence soon after the Second World War, its oppressed people were amongst the poorest and least educated in the world. There were less than twenty university graduates amongst them. The discovery of oil beneath their desert homeland brought a sudden invasion of technology and money.

Libya is on the coast of North Africa and much of it is within the Sahara Desert. It borders Tunisia and Algeria to the west, Chad and Niger to the south, and Egypt and Sudan are to the east and south-east. For a country with a landmass of 679,500 square miles, it has a small population. In 2011 it was estimated to be 6,276,632.

Its history is fascinating. The ancient Greeks, the Phoenicians and the Romans all established colonies in Libya. They built the cities of Cyrene, Sabratha, Oea (Tripoli) and Leptis Magna, the remains of which still grace its Mediterranean coast. These great civilisations were followed by the expansion of the Arab caliphate into North Africa and Spain. In its turn the caliphate faded away, leaving behind the Bedouin tribes which still range the Libyan hinterland with their herds and flocks.

In 1551, after a short rule, the Knights of St John were evicted from Tripoli by the Ottoman Turks led by the corsair Dragut. Subsequently, Libya became an important province of the Ottoman Empire and, for a while, was ruled by the cruel and dissolute Karamanli dynasty of slave-trading corsairs. Their harassment of the merchant shipping of the newly formed United Sates of America resulted in a war which lasted from 1801 to 1805.

The Ottomans ruled Libya from 1551 to 1912, when the Italians pushed them out. There followed a period of Italian colonisation, which became appallingly brutal. The Libyan tribes eventually rebelled against their colonial masters. Led by the teacher and soldier Omar Mukhtar, they fought a classic guerrilla war in the green mountains of East Libya. However, the rebellion failed and Omar Mukhtar was hanged.

In September 1940, thinking the Germans were about to win the Second World War, Mussolini sent an Italian army from Libya into Egypt to threaten the British. There followed the war in the Western Desert, in which the Germans also became involved. The legendary Desert Fox and the Desert Rats fought on Libyan soil, as did the independent units, the SAS, the Long Range Desert Group and Popski's Private Army. The British and Commonwealth 8th Army toppled the Italian Empire in Libya and replaced it with a British administration.

The British were tired and impoverished after the war, so they helped the United Nations to combine the three provinces of Tripolitania, Cyrenaica and the Fezzan into an independent Kingdom of Libya, ruled by the sometime Amir of Cyrenaica, Sayyid Muhammad al Idris as-Senussi.

In its early days, the Kingdom of Libya was dependent on the British and US forces which occupied it under a treaty. When geologists detected oil in the desert, Libya began to change. The adventurous days of searching for oil and the coming of the oil barons, such as Nelson Bunker Hunt and Armand Hammer, were too much for King Idris, who lived in a modest palace near Tobruk and preferred quiet contemplation rather than vigorous kingship. His courtiers descended into corruption and bribery while the great oil fields developed in the desert.

To the surprise of both the UK and Egypt, a young Libyan army officer called Muammar Gaddafi staged a brilliant coup on 1 September 1969, when the king was absent in Turkey on sick leave. Gaddafi and his Revolutionary Command Council nationalised British Petroleum and rewrote the contracts of the other great oil companies. He removed the British and US forces from his country and led it into a flirtation with the communist bloc.

Under his rule Libya became a pariah state, harbouring terrorists from nearly every dissident group in the world. He aggravated the USA and forced its government to launch a pre-emptive air strike against him on 15 April 1986.

His acquisition of mustard gas and his attempts to develop other weapons of mass destruction caused much consternation. His support for the IRA, the killing of PC Yvonne Fletcher and the apparent role of Libyans in the destruction of Pan American World Airways flight PA103 in December 1988 angered the British.

His rule became more and more autocratic and his people rose up against him on 17 February 2011.

1

The Greeks, the Romans and the Garamantes

Libya is rich in the ruins of ancient Roman and Greek cities. In the south there are signs of a lost African civilisation, which the Romans called the Garamantes.

Even when these civilisations were at the height of their powers they were mostly separated by geographical barriers. The west was Roman, the east was Greek and the south, African. The three Libyan provinces of Tripolitania, Cyrenaica and the Fezzan, which arose amongst the remains of these civilisations, were influenced by their ancient predecessors. The Gaddafi regime abolished the old provincial names, calling Tripolitania West Libya, Cyrenaica East Libya and the Fezzan South Libya. However, the provinces live on in spirit to make it difficult to unify modern Libya.

The civil war that broke out in Libya on 17 February 2011 reflected deep differences between the old provinces of Tripolitania and Cyrenaica. Apart from the physical separation by the inhospitable desert region of the Sirtica, the history of the two regions has been very different. Greece and Egypt have long influenced Cyrenaicans and Carthage and Rome Tripolitanians. The remote desert province of the Fezzan has forever been involved with sub-Saharan Africa by reasons of human kinship and the trans-Saharan trade in slaves, gold and wild animals. The people of the three provinces are therefore separated by differences that have persisted for thousands of years.

The border between Tripolitania and Cyrenaica meets the coast at a legendary spot called the Altars of the Philaeni. It was said that the Phoenician founders of Tripoli were so jealous of their trade that they excluded the Greeks of Libya Pentapolis, in what was known until recently as Cyrenaica. The place that marked the border between them became a bone of contention.

Legend has it that the Phoenicians and the Greeks, after a number of skirmishes, agreed to establish the frontier between their two territories by means of a foot race. Runners were to set off towards each other from Carthage in the west and Cyrene in the east. Where they met was to mark the frontier.

The Phoenician team, the Philaeni brothers, reached a point in the desert at the southern extremity of the Gulf of Sirte before they met the Greeks. The Greeks were angry because they expected their team to get further, and so they accused the Philaeni brothers of cheating. The Phoenicians denied it, so both parties agreed to settle the dispute by burying the Philaeni brothers alive to mark the frontier. Two mounds were said to have been built over the graves, on which the Altars of the Philaeni were erected. This is an unlikely story, but one that reflects the intensity of the original dispute.

In the twentieth century, Mussolini built a triumphal arch on the border as a monument to his African conquests. This pompous edifice looked similar to the arch at the top of Park Lane in London. British Second World War soldiers, whose dry sense of humour was legendary, called it Marble Arch, so it was known thus throughout the 8th Army and the name stuck.[1] My wife and I drove past the Marble Arch on our way from Tripoli to Benghazi. It had a large bronze human figure somehow appended to the side. One of its big toes had been cut off. Sometime later I saw a grotesque bronze object on the desk of an Englishman in Benghazi. It was the missing toe, which he had cut off and was using as an ashtray.

For more than four centuries, the two provinces were joined under Roman rule. There was a common language, a cohesive government and a common legal system. Ruins of the great cities still grace the Libyan shores of the Mediterranean and have within them common and unifying features – pubic baths, stadia, theatres, art and architecture – found throughout the Roman Empire. Even so, the ruins of Tripolitania are clearly Punic in character, whilst those of Cyrenaica are unmistakably Greek.

The archaeological and historical evidence tells us that Christianity spread across the two provinces in the second

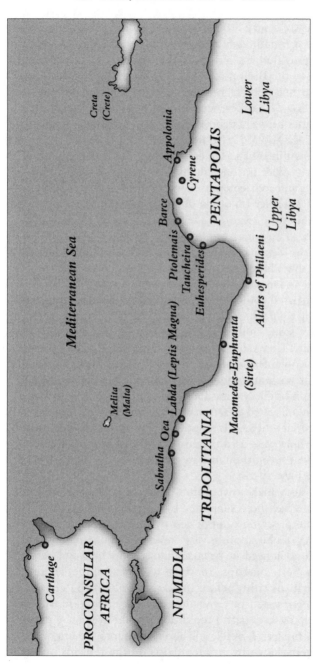

The Punic and Greek cities of Libya. Sabratha, Oea and Leptis Magna became Roman cities after the Punic wars. The Greek cities of Libya Pentapolis were eventually taken over by Rome. (The legendary Altars of Philaeni were erected to mark the boundary between the Punic east and the Greek west.)

century AD. It may have been spread by the Jewish communities and found ready converts amongst the slaves and the
indigenous Berbers. However, the churches of Tripolitania
looked to the Bishop of Rome for leadership, whilst those
of Cyrenaica were in the diocese of the Coptic Patriarch of
Alexandria. The differences in religious observance created
animosities between people during hard economic times and
often, as they do today, led to warfare.

My own interest in the early history of Libya grew out of
familiarity with the ancient ruins and contact with anthropologists and archaeologists working on such diverse subjects
as the possible Jewish origin of the cave dwellers in the Gebel
Nefusa and the export trade from the ancient Greek port
of Tokra (Taucheira). Sometimes I was asked to help them
during the 'digging' seasons, though in practical ways, such as
solving those little local difficulties with authorities that were
endemic in Libya and probably still are.

My belated apologies are extended to the charming and
forgiving team which, in the 1960s, went to Cyrene to explore
the huge stone-built pipelines connecting that city with its
hinterland. They came to me to hire or borrow a Land Rover,
which I obtained for them from my friend Mohammed al
Abbar. It was not a good vehicle on which to depend in the
remote and slightly hazardous region in which they worked,
but I was obligated to al Abbar and their troubles with it were
a by-product thereof. Interestingly, this team concluded that
the pipelines were used to transport olive oil for the city from
the olive groves; though how this might have worked was
always a mystery to me.

This story makes two points. The first is that the ancient
cites must have been supported by large and efficient agricultural enterprises, now lost or destroyed. The second is that the
'currency of obligations' is very powerful in modern Libya and
is a factor that needs to be taken into account by Westerners.

It is best, perhaps, to start with the three ancient
Tripolitanian cities before looking briefly at the classical
Greek civilisation in Cyrenaica. There is method in this. It
will help to understand the differences between the provinces of modern Libya. It will also lead us into the important
work being done by archaeologists on the remains of lost

civilisations. We will surely hear more of this work when it is safe for archaeologists to return to Libya after the civil war.

The Phoenicians and the Garamantes

A question that modern visitors to the three cities, Sabratha, Oea (Tripoli) and Leptis Magna, often ask is why they were first established so close together on the Mediterranean shore of Tripolitania. The visitors are puzzled because the three of them, existing together in such close proximity, would have outstripped the natural resources of the coast or its immediate hinterland.

The question forces us to venture into the insecure realms of conjecture and hypothesis. We know that the three cites originated as Phoenician trading posts, which were taken over by the Carthaginians, whose great city, Carthage, came to dominate the coast. The Phoenicians and the Carthaginians were traders first and last. They guarded their trade secrets with paranoid zeal, leaving few clues for archaeologists to unravel. To add to our problems, the city of Carthage was totally destroyed by the Romans in 146 BC and with it all the records that might have helped us as historians.

Since we believe that trade outweighed politics for the Carthaginians, we might suggest that the three cities were established primarily as trading posts. We might go further and argue that Sabratha, Oea and Leptis Magna were founded by three separate trading houses, all engaged in the same trade.

Business must have been very good indeed to support three such emporia. The maritime carrying trade, that is the shipping and the trading of goods around the Mediterranean, would not have been sufficient. We must look elsewhere for a reason.

It may lie to the south, in what was once the Fezzan. In ancient times it was the territory of the Garamantes, a long-lost people to whom some, though significantly not all, attribute the rock paintings that still remain in good condition to the wonder and puzzlement of those rare and lucky people who ventured into the arid wastes of South Libya.

One other recurrent traveller's tale about the Fezzan was that its early inhabitants used chariots. Visitors to Tripoli museum today will find there a replica of a chariot believed to have been used by the enigmatic Garamantes. They were said by Strabo to breed 100,000 foals per year. This suggests that the terrain was suitable for their use. Horses, which need frequent access to water and plenty of fodder, are not suitable for long-distance travel in desert conditions. The implication is that access to water and fodder was widely available when these chariots were in use and the intensive horse-breeding programme was active.

Perhaps one of the most surprising references to the ancient civilisation in the Fezzan is this, found in a letter written in January 1789 by Miss Tully, the sister of the British consul to the Karamanli court of Tripoli. In it she describes the Prince of Fezzan, and something of his kingdom, thus:

> The Prince of Fezzan's turban, instead of being large and of white muslin like those of Tripoli, was composed of a black and gold shawl, wound tightly several times round the head, and a long and curiously wrought shawl hung low over the left shoulder. The baracan was white and perfectly transparent; and his arms were handsome, with a profusion of gold and silver chains hanging from them.
>
> He told us his country is the most fertile and beautiful in the world, having himself seen no part of the globe but Africa; and Fezzan esteemed amongst the richest of its kingdoms.
>
> In the Fezzan there are still vestiges of magnificent buildings, and a number of curiously vaulted caves of immense size, supposed to have been Roman granaries. But it requires a more enlightened mind than that of the Moor and the Arab to discover their origin.[2]

Miss Tully, whose work is discussed elsewhere in this short history, was describing a visit to Tripoli by the Prince of Fezzan during the Karamanli regency. That she was observant enough to note the profusion of gold which adorned the prince, and that the Fezzan still boasted a number of mysterious and notable ruins, is not surprising. She was, as we shall see, an excellent observer and most thorough in her research. The African source of gold, so ostentatiously adorning Miss Tully's

Fezzanese guests, was to become one of the great mysteries of the late Georgian age in Britain.

In more peaceful times, before the present civil war in Libya, archaeologists were engaged in studying the numerous and intriguing cave paintings and also attempting to bring the Garamantes into better focus. Thanks to David Mattingly and his team from the University of Leicester and Andrew Wilson of the University of Oxford, we now know that the Garamantes were able to tap into the vast aquifer of water deep under the Saharan desert; the same water that has been exploited in modern times by Gaddafi in his 'Great Man Made River' scheme, of which more soon.

The archaeologists have concluded that the Garamantes constructed almost 1,000 miles of underground tunnels and shafts, known locally as foggara, to get at the artesian water. These are the vaulted caves mentioned by Miss Tully. We may also conclude that they would have used many slaves to construct the tunnels. Others have noted that they silted-up frequently and needed constant cleaning. It is clear that the abundant supply of water was used to support an extensive and sophisticated agriculture and a large population.

The archaeologists believe that by AD 105 the Garamantian state covered 70,000 square miles of the Fezzan and that there were eight towns and many settlements. (I understand that David Mattingly has concluded that the water ran out in the end, causing the civilisation to wither away; a salutary lesson for us all. Others, Robert Graves amongst them, argue that the Garamantians merely left for new lands elsewhere.)[3]

Studies of the Garamantian capital, now the town called Germa, tell us that it was guarded by six towers and that it may have had a market square used for trading horses, which were sold to the Romans. It also served as a transit stop for caravans, probably from the south, on their way along what is now known as the Garamantes Road, which terminated near Tripoli.

More than 50,000 pyramidal tombs have been discovered in the Fezzan, including one thought to have been for royalty at Ahramat al-Hattia. There is a museum in Germa in which are a number of artefacts, including some well-preserved cave art in which giraffes and a large ox are depicted. These animals, which we now associate with East and South Africa, were clearly able to survive in the Fezzan when these paintings were made.

Trade with the Garamantes was not just the possible, but the principal reason for founding the three large emporia so close together on the coast of the Lesser Sirte.

The Romans

The Punic wars are familiar enough to need only a few words here. They ended when the Romans razed Carthage to the ground in 146 BC. For our purposes, it was Caesar's victory over Juba, the Berber leader, at Thapsus in 46 BC and the death of Ptolemy, the son of Juba II, which led the Romans to expand their control over the whole of the North Africa littoral from Leptis Magna in the east to the Atlantic. They occupied Sabratha, Oea (Tripoli) and Leptis and continued to trade with the Garamantes.

Leptis, called Leptis Magna to distinguish it from Leptis Minor in Tunisia, was captured by the Romans in 46 BC. They levied the city for 3 million pounds of olive oil, indicating that there were extensive olive groves in the region.

Leptis Magna was to achieve fame and fortune when one of its sons, Septimus Severus, became Emperor of Rome. After his accession, he caused a great deal of money to be poured into improving his home town, and some glorious buildings were erected. It is situated on a small natural harbour at the head of the wadi, about 120km to the east of Tripoli.

Septimus Severus was one of the Roman emperors to make a donation of olive oil to the Roman citizens, in addition to the traditional corn donations. In his excellent book, *The Corn Supply of Ancient Rome*, Geoffrey Rickman suggests that the three cities, Sabratha, Oea and Leptis Magna, were more prominent as olive oil suppliers to Rome, though they contributed a great deal of the corn supply. Olive trees have deep roots and are able to reduce their water loss through their leaves. They do, however, need a long time to grow and produce fruit. Political stability is necessary before people invest in cultivating them.[4]

The Romans pushed their frontier inland to the southern-most slopes of the Gebel Nefusa, and in doing so came into conflict with the nomadic tribes that migrated from the desert into the Gebel each year to pasture their animals. The tribes, which hitherto acknowledged the Garamantes as their masters, now found themselves dominated by the aggressive Romans, who were not happy to allow them past their new frontiers.

It was also inevitable that the Romans would fall out with the Garamantes, and they did so in typical fashion. At the end of the first century BC they sent a punitive expedition under the leadership of their proconsul, Lucius Cornelius Balbus, a native of Spain. The expedition took the Garamantes by sur-prise; the possibility of an army reaching them from the coast had seemed unlikely to them.

Balbus was accorded a triumph in Rome for his efforts, a rare honour for a foreigner. It was, after all, a notable feat of arms to take an army deep into the Sahara and conduct a sur-prise attack on a formidable enemy, capture his capital city, a number of other towns and, most usefully, one of his outlying oases, Ghadames, thus controlling his northbound trade.

Further friction between the Romans and the Garamantes occurred in AD 17, when a Roman-trained Libyan soldier called Tacfarinas raised a revolt in the neighbouring Greek province of Cyrenaica. This spread into Tripolitania and began to affect the Roman provinces to the west. So serious was the revolt that the Romans moved the 9th Spanish Legion across to support the Legio III Augusta, which was already stationed in North Africa.

Tacfarinas, however, defied the Romans for seven years. In a move not uncommon in modern history, the Roman emperor withdrew the Spanish legion for work elsewhere, just when they were most needed in Libya. Tacfarinas, as would his modern counterpart today, saw this as an admission of weak-ness by the Romans and persuaded the Garamantes to join him in removing the occupying power. Tacfarinas was finally killed in battle and his revolt collapsed, as they often do when fomented and led by a single personality.[5]

The Garamantes, realising that the Romans would be less than pleased that they had supported Tacfarinas, sent an embassy to Rome and sued for peace. However, they backed the wrong horse in AD 69, when Oea and Leptis Magna fell out and began to fight. The Garamantes foolishly pitched in on the side of Oea. The Roman proconsul, Valerius Festus, hastened to intervene. He freed Leptis Magna and pursued the Garamantes into the Sahara. They had thought they could escape by filling in the wells on the old Garamantian Road with sand, thus making it impossible for troops to follow them. They misjudged Festus. He discovered a new route through the desert and attacked them in their homeland.

The new route was described as being short and fast. It was probably the one from Oea through Gharian and Mizda, which was later to be marked by Roman milestones. That it was unknown to the Garamantes is puzzling, as was their rapid U-turn in foreign policy resulting in a rapprochement with the Romans. Perhaps they realised that the Romans had found a means of projecting their military power across the desert.

There are other perplexing and interesting events. In AD 100 or thereabouts, the Romans mounted some peaceful expeditions to the south of the Fezzan. One such, led by Julius Maternus, was probably to the Tebesti Mountains. These expeditions could not have been mounted without the assistance, or at least the connivance, of the Garamantes.

The speed with which Festus invaded the Fezzan, and the ability of the Romans to mount long-range expeditions in arid country, point to a striking and effective innovation in logistics. It is most likely that this was the use of camels, as it is this animal alone that could have so effectively rendered the inhospitable Sahara accessible to them.

The Romans made brilliant mosaics. In the ancient Roman port of Ostia there is one that illustrates some of the fauna of the province of Africa. It was probably made for a merchant specialising in the import of beasts for the Roman games. The records show that this was a lucrative business. Caesar once supplied 400 lions to be killed by gladiators in one orgy. Pompey upstaged him by supplying 600. Augustus is said to have caused the slaughter of 3,500 animals in twenty-six shows and Titus celebrated the inauguration of the Colosseum by seeing off 9,000 animals, and probably a few gladiators.

Elephants were not used in these orgies of slaughter. Perhaps even the Romans recoiled from the sight of their death agonies. However, they coveted ivory and they enjoyed a dish made with the cartilage from an elephant's trunk. This must have led to the slaughter of not a few of these precious beasts.[6]

It is clear that the magnitude of slaughter is only partially illustrated by the records. The total number of animals sacrificed in an attempt to satisfy the jaded tastes of the Roman masses must have been astronomical. Some of the wild animals were from Asia and Egypt, but the great majority came from the Roman province of Africa, which is roughly Tunisia and Tripolitania.

The 2011 civil war in Libya had, at its core, the events in the Cyrenaican (East Libyan) town of Benghazi between 17 and 20 February. The towns of Cyrenaica, Derna and Tobruk also made common cause with their Benghaziot friends, and the whole of the Cyrenaican littoral, at least as far west as Ajadabia, came under anti-Gaddafi influence and remain so as I write. The historical difference between Cyrenaica and Tripolitania appears to be little understood amongst present-day pundits.

The Greeks

First of all, Libya, the Greek name for the original inhabitants of what we might now call Cyrenaica, was chosen as the name for the newly independent country in 1953 because Tripolitania had definite Italian overtones and thus was too closely associated with the late colonists who were, by that time, much disliked.

In 631 BC the fertile land west of Egypt, now known as the Gebel Akhdar, received a colony from the Greek island of Thera, now Santorini, which had become overpopulated and was in the throes of a famine. The Therans were soon joined by other colonists from the Aegean islands.

The colony was successful and gave rise to four daughter colonies: Euhesperides (later Berenice and now Benghazi); Appolonia (the port of Cyrene on the coast below the great city itself); Taucheira (now called Tokra, the ruins of which guard the Tokra Pass up into the Gebel Akhdar); and Ptolemais. These five communities together were sometimes known as Libya Pentapolis.

The Greek colonists were sometimes at war with the white-skinned Libyans, with whom there was also intermarriage. In addition, they were involved in wars in Egypt and on one occasion set off a revolution against the Pharaoh Hopra. There was also friction with the Carthaginians, who barred them from entering the colonists' territory. Cyrene and its daughter colonies remained a monarchy under the dynasty of its founder, Battus the First, until a republic was founded in or about 450 BC.

A famous ceramic vase from Sparta has a panel on which has been painted a representation of the King of Cyrene sitting under an awning, supervising the weighing of agricultural produce. The picture includes a monkey, now clearly extinct in the Gebel Akhdar, and a gecko, now abundant therein.[7]

The level of civilisation in Cyrene was notably high as the great ruins, still seen in the Gebel Akhdar, amply testify. The fertile region that surrounds it was brilliantly cultivated and supplied the Greek city states with livestock, wine, apples and olive oil. One famous export was silphium, a plant which had a very restricted habitat in the Gebel Akhdar and grew nowhere else. There is still some speculation as to why the plant was so important that it was eventually used to extinction. It may have been a laxative. Otherwise it may have been the Cyrenaican version of the 'morning-after' pill, a use that would have created a ferocious demand.

The five cites of Libya Pentapolis were unable to combine for any length of time and thus were vulnerable to invasion. Perhaps that is why they were unable to prevent the Persian King Cambrensis III taking it into his empire in 525 BC. For two centuries the five cities remained part of the Persian Empire.

They emerged into history again when Alexander the Great was about to make his famous journey to consult the Oracle of Zeus-Ammon in the remote oasis of Siwa, close to the Libyan border. He had concluded that he was a god, it seems, and needed the oracle to confirm his aspirations. He first took the coast road towards Libya from his newly founded Alexandria, and was met by an embassy from Cyrene, no doubt keen to make their peace with him. After this, Alexander turned south to make his near-fatal pilgrimage across the desert to Siwa, when he and his followers were lost for a while in a fierce sandstorm.

Alexander the Great died in 323 BC, only eight years after his armies arrived in Cyrenaica. His empire was divided between his Macedonian generals. So it was in 323 BC that Cyrene and Egypt went to Ptolemy, who founded a great dynasty of Greek pharaohs which lasted over 200 years. In 96 BC the Greek influence in Cyrene began to dwindle, and the last Greek ruler, Ptolemy XII Apion, left it to the Romans in his will. It became a Roman province and, for a while, one of Caesar's assassins, Brutus, was dispatched there as governor to get him out of Rome.

It became involved in the great power struggle between Octavian and Mark Antony when the latter gave it as a wedding present to Cleopatra the Great as part of the restoration of much of the old Ptolemaic Empire. It must have been interesting in Cyrenaica when Antony stationed no less than four of his legions there. They eventually reneged on him and went over to Octavian, who, of course, won the great sea battle of Actium. The defeated Antony and Cleopatra famously committed suicide. Cyrene was given to Cleopatra's only daughter, Cleopatra Celene, who was eventually married to Prince Juba. He had lived in Rome since he was 4 and was, nominally at least, client King of Numidia.

In the end, Cyrenaica and Crete were combined into a single province under Roman rule, which lasted 300 years.

The fall and ruin of the great civilisations in Libya was to be followed, eventually, by the arrival from the east of two Bedouin tribes whose influence was profound.

2

The Arab Invasion
The True Bedouin Arrive

*In AD 643 the Muslim general Amir ibn al 'As invaded Cyrenaica
and soon afterwards Tripolitania. Uqba bin Nafi moved towards
Fezzan in AD 663 and took Germa. Afterwards, Libya was no longer
part of the Dar al Harb (the House of War), but part of the Islamic
world, the Dar al Islam.*

*After 1050 two true Arab Bedouin tribes from the Nejd migrated
belligerently into Libya. They were the Beni Sulaim and the Beni
Hilal. Their descendants followed their customs and way of life in
Libya until recently and they still exert great influence.*

*The trans-Saharan trade, notably in slaves, passed through the
Fezzan to Tripoli. The Norman kings of Sicily and the Catholic cru-
saders of Spain both briefly occupied Tripoli in their turn.*

The decline of Roman Libya was signalled by economic
troubles exported from Rome itself. Christianity grew in
importance and sectarian tension caused some discord.
Greater challengers came from the Sirtica. In AD 363, a group
of tribes from this region exploded out of their homeland
and raided the hinterland of Leptis Magna. The Sirtican tribes
were so successful with their first attack that they tried again a
few years later and wantonly destroyed farms and estates.

The Vandals thrust themselves into Libyan history in AD 429,
when they were invited there to aid a Roman general in a
revolt against imperial Rome. They outstayed their welcome
and enhanced their reputation for destructive campaigning by
destroying the walls of Sabratha and Leptis Magna, though not
of Oea. Their occupation of the three cities was short-sighted
because they neglected the defence works that protected the

settled hinterland and allowed Berber tribes to infiltrate and destroy hard-won farmlands and estates.

The Byzantines removed the Vandals from Tripolitania, and, for a while, exercised a less than welcome suzerainty. Byzantine control in Tripolitania was confined to the coast. They built walled towns, strongholds, fortified farms and watchtowers, which show that their hold was none too secure. The region's prosperity had shrunk under Vandal domination, and the old Roman political and social order could not be restored.

They were more successful in Cyrenaica and held back the decline of the five cities. The Byzantine Emperor Justinian was particularly diligent and active in this regard. Perhaps this was because Cyrenaica had been included in the Greek eastern half and Tripolitania in the Latin half when the Roman Empire was divided in AD 395. Cyrenaica was thus more compatible with the Byzantines and survived under their protection for longer. Byzantine rule in Libya did prolong a semblance of Roman civilisation for a while. However, the decline was inexorable, and by the end of the sixth century it was almost complete.

The detailed history of the decline and fall of the ancient civilisations in Libya is complicated and fascinating. It is described brilliantly by John Wright in his comprehensive *History of Libya* and in more detail in the publications of the Society of Libyan Studies. Others may discern amongst the details events that have a bearing on modern Libya. In the meantime, there follows a summary of the notes I made whilst travelling around Libya in the 1960s. My untutored reaction to the ruined Greek and Roman cities is probably echoed by visitors today.

Of the five original Greek cites of Cyrenaica, few have been continuously occupied into modern times. Cyrene declined in wealth as its port, Appolonia, rose in importance. However, it flourished for some considerable time, as the remains of five Byzantine churches and a Byzantine palace testify.

The remains of Tokra are not extensive. It was a port of some importance and, at the time of my visit, caves nearby still contained amphora, probably for shipping wine. The site of Barce is now occupied by the town of el Marj, which suffered an earthquake in 1963. The quake hit the town just as the inhabitants were eating their evening meal during the Ramadan fast and there was a heavy death toll caused by falling masonry.

Euhesperides fell into decline and was frequently attacked by Libyan tribes. It was replaced at some time by a new wave of Greek settlers, who built a town somewhat westward of the old city, but the Vandals reduced it and it fell out of history for a while. The modern city of Benghazi occupies this new site.

In Tripolitania, Roman Oea is now largely buried under the modern city of Tripoli. The Arch of Marcus Aurelius remains to remind the casual visitor of its past. Even now, farmers in the region plough up hoards of Roman coins. This reminds us that times were not always peaceful in the region, for people tend to bury their money when they lose confidence in their government. Perhaps these Tripolitanian coin hoards were buried when the fierce tribes from the Sirtica attacked the three cities, or when the Vandals invaded as the Roman Empire fell apart. The ruins of Sabratha and Leptis Magna remain as silent reminders that it was once possible to support a large population on the Mediterranean shore of Tripolitania.

We are now reaching one of the key events in the history of modern Libya. Amir ibn al 'As, during the caliphate of Umar, conquered Syria and Egypt. In AD 643, he invaded Cyrenaica. He made Barce his headquarters and that is why Cyrenaica is called Barca by the Arabs. The Arabs went on to attack the Byzantine Emperor Gregory's city of Tripoli between AD 647 and 648. It was taken when the emperor was killed beneath the city walls.

The normal route from Cyrenaica to Tripolitania was by sea across the Gulf of Sirte, but the Arab generals led their troops across the challenging desert region of the Sirtica. To get an army across the 300 miles of desert was a notable military feat, probably accomplished for the first time. There is a simple reason for this and for the notable mobility of the Arab armies of this period. It was the Arabian camel, the dromedary, which has an array of adaptations that allow it to carry loads for long periods without water and with a minimum of food in arid conditions.

Its hump, a unique storage system for fat, can be metabolised during starvation before the animal's body calls on muscle protein. Its nose, eyes and ears are protected from blowing sand, and its teeth and lips are adapted to eat tough desert fodder. Its kidneys are very efficient and its stomach stores water in its lining. It walks well on soft sand and, unusually for a mammal, its body temperature fluctuates, enabling it to withstand wide changes in temperature. Its smell disconcerts horses, its momentum knocks troops over effectively and it is reasonably responsive to skilled human management. As a last resort, it is edible and some say water may be recovered from its stomach lining. All this makes it a potent cavalry weapon and a military beast of burden in arid regions. Its use by the Arab armies allowed them to travel great distances and conquer vast territories.

In AD 663 the Caliph Umar then sent Uqba bin Nafi to take Fezzan. Within the span of about seventy years the whole of North Africa was in Muslim hands. This is, of course, the opening move in the establishment of the western expansion of great Islamic caliphates into Spain, Sicily and the south of France. It is this caliphate to which the militant Islamists of today hark back and which they aim to re-establish and expand. It was at its height between AD 786 and 709, in the reign of Harun al Rashid, whose capital was Damascus. It was during this time that the stories called *The Book of One Thousand and One Nights* were collected, giving us Ali Baba, Sinbad and Aladdin.

The legacy of it all is best illustrated by this succinct analysis:

> The Arab sense of bygone splendour is superb. One cannot understand the modern Arab if one lacks a perspective feeling for this. In the gulf between him and, for instance, the modern American, a matter of prime significance has been precisely the deep difference between a society with a memory of past greatness, and one with a sense of present greatness.[1]

The history of the Arab invasion of Libya and of the subsequent rise and fall of Islamic caliphates, which were to rule it for many years, is complex. From our point of view, it is the effect of the Arab conquest on modern Libya that is important.

Before embarking on a discussion about modern Libya, we might remind ourselves that the period between AD 656 and 661, roughly speaking, is one of lasting importance for Islam: it was when the struggle for supremacy was waged between prominent heads of several families of the Prophet Muhammad's tribe, the Quarish. The upshot was that the faithful divided into three subdivisions which persist today. The orthodox Sunni form the largest division. The next largest division consists of the followers of Ali ibn Abi Talib – cousin and son-in-law of the Prophet. This division is known as the Shiat Ali (Shia or Shiites). A little-known breakaway division, called the Kharijites, was formed by some purists who were unhappy about the schism. The modern Libyans adhere to the Sunni or orthodox division of Islam.

The Arab Muslims who first conquered Cyrenaica and Tripolitania were soldiers who tended to occupy the towns and leave the surroundings largely alone. In the hinterland, the indigenous Berbers maintained much of their culture, language, religion and writing; the writing, incidentally, is obscure and was used and passed on by females.

There was an interesting interlude when Tripoli was occupied by Europeans and survived as a city state. The Fezzan, as a quasi-state controlling the trans-Saharan trade routes, was connected to the invasion of Tripoli by the Norman kings of Sicily. In 1130 a group of Norman adventurers captured Sicily and founded a kingdom. They were headed by the de Hauteville family, which came from the Cotentin Peninsular. Roger de Hauteville, as Roger II, was King of Sicily between 1130 and 1154. His famous admiral, George of Antioch, captured Tripoli in 1146. This was during the period of the crusades, but not part of that military adventure. Despite pressure, Roger II adroitly sidestepped the second crusade because he ruled a kingdom of many Muslims.

For him Tripoli served two purposes. One was strategic because it gave him control over the narrow seaways between the western and eastern Mediterranean. The second reason was that it gave him access to the trans-Saharan and the carrier trade of Tripoli. The main route for trade through the Fezzan was the ancient Garamantian trail.

Roger's successor, William I, lost Tripoli, perhaps because his interests lay elsewhere, but it remained a powerful trading centre through which the trans-Saharan trade flowed for many years and travellers commented on its prosperity and cleanliness. It was also a centre for the business of piracy.

Moorish Iberia began a period of decline from 1130 and in 1492 came the ascendancy of the Christians, Isabella of Castile and Ferdinand of Aragon. Crusading Spain began to invade North Africa. Don Pedro of Navarre landed 6,000 men in Tripoli in July 1510 and took the town in a bloody battle.

In the eleventh century Libya, aside from Tripoli, entered a dark age from which it still suffers. In 1050 and 1051 came the Hilalian migration. Two Arab tribes that came from the Nejd, the Beni Sulaim and the Beni Hilal, had been driven into Egypt as a result of a thwarted attempt to enter Arabia. They had settled in Upper Egypt but were true Bedouin, with a way of life that was not appreciated by a population amongst whom they failed to co-exist.

The Fatimid Caliph of Egypt encouraged the two tribes to move westward into Cyrenaica, Tripolitania and Tunis to squeeze out the indigenous Berbers, who were attempting to assert their independence. The new invaders occupied much of Libya with notable savagery. There was a difference, however. It was a belligerent migration, rather than a military conquest.

There are no records of the number of Beni Sulaim or Beni Hilal who took part in this migration. The tribes moved, lock, stock and barrel, though in this case it would be better to say 'tent, stock and camel'. The Bedouin are adapted to migrant pastoralism. The Beni Hilal and the Beni Sulaim were capable of moving slowly over great distances with their adaptable sheep, goats and camels. The camel provided transport and was useful militarily. Their tents are readily erected or struck by females with long experience of transhumance. In this way, the Hilalian migration brought not only whole families but also an intact and conservative culture into Libya.

The Beni Sulaim, the senior tribe, found Cyrenaica congenial and many of them settled there. The Beni Hilal drove on westwards. Five of the Tripolitanian tribes are said to descend from them. The historian John Wright has suggested that the Beni Sulaim had finally completed their settlement of the northern part of Cyrenaica in the 1060s.

The descendants of the Beni Sulaim are still spread over a large area in Egypt and Tunisia. There are two tribes that claim descent from them in Tripolitania. However, those occupying modern Cyrenaica founded nine famous aristocratic Bedouin tribes. These nine, the so-called Sa'adi tribes, are divided into two branches, the Jibarna and the Harabi.

The Jibarna tribes are the Awaqir, the Magharba, the Abid and the Arafa. The Harabi are the Abaidat, the Hasa, the Fayid, the Bara'asa and the Darsa. These nine tribes have pushed out a number of other Beni Sulaim, such as the Aulad Ali who now occupy much of the Western Desert of Egypt.[2]

Whilst the ancient history of the Beni Sulaim is unknown to the great majority of people of the nine tribes, they are fanatical genealogists and will recount their perceived line of descent from the so-called mother of the nine tribes, the eponymous Sa'ad. That they all claim descent from one mother is important because, when faced with a common enemy, the Sa'adi tribes make common cause. This point is revisited later in the discussion about the Senussi wars against the Italians.

The nine tribes own their own homelands by right of conquest. They are, in this regard, freemen and are referred to as Hurr (free or noble). Anyone who can successfully claim descent from the founding mother Sa'ad is a nobleman or Hurr by birth, and has the right to the natural resources of his homeland. Each of the nine tribes are divided and subdivided, with each section having the right to its homeland (its *watan*). There are other tribes that are not descended from the founding ancestress Sa'adi. They are known as the Marabtin, which roughly translated means 'tied', and they are sometimes referred to as client tribes. These are tribes do not own land, but use it by permission of the Sa'adi tribes and pay dues in kind.

It is time to ask how relevant the Hilalian migration of Libya is today. As E.E. Evans-Pritchard wrote of their descendants when he encountered them in 1943: '[they are] as Arab as any people in the world, proud Tammim and Quarash not excepted.' The tribes that claim descent from the Hilal and Beni Sulaim had, until recently, 'the same tented, pastoral, way of life, the same social organisation, the same laws and customs and manners, and the same values'.[3]

I argue that there are two main reasons to take careful note of the Hilalian migration. The first is that the customs of

Gaddafi's tribe, the Gaddadfa, were imported from the Nejd by the Beni Hilal and the Beni Sulaim if Evans-Pritchard is right.

The second point is of wider significance. The ancient cites of Tripolitania and Libya Pantapolis were clearly supported by extensive and intensive agriculture. As you fly south from Tripoli you can still see the limits of Roman cultivation outlined by traces of the three defensive walls they built to protect the cultivated land. Land-bound travellers are struck by the profusion of ancient olive oil storage tanks, water cisterns and other signs of careful water conservation and agricultural workings. There are abundant signs of deforestation. To add weight to these observations, historians of Rome and Greece tell us that olive oil and corn were exported in great quantities from Libya.

Hated as they were, the Italian colonists of the twentieth century were introducing into Libya the labour-intensive farming methods from their side of the Mediterranean. These methods require years of small-scale water conservation, ploughing and plant breeding. For example, olive trees need time to grow and bear fruit. It is possible to develop and maintain Mediterranean-style agriculture in parts of Libya, but it requires skills which also take time to learn.

The development and maintenance of a large urban civilisation requires a number of social, scientific, entrepreneurial and mechanical skills. The Libyan people lost these skills at some time and the world moved on.

The near-contemporary geographers and historians were stuck by the devastation caused by Beni Hilal and Beni Sulaim. The fourteenth-century Tunisian historian, Ibn Khaldun, likened them to a swarm of locusts devouring the whole country over which they passed. Later historians, E.W. Bovill for example, state that the most serious consequence of the devastation they caused was that enormous areas went permanently out of cultivation. As Bovill says, 'directly or through their herds, these wild Arabs also destroyed most of the forests, thus creating the shortage of timber, which in later times had serious consequences to their descendants'.[4] If we accept these two assertions, it is clearer that the Beni Sulaim and the Beni Hilal choked off technical, scientific, philosophical and political progress in Libya. It was certainly not the first Arab invaders who caused the decline, because culture and civilisation flourished in many other countries they took over.

The Libyan Bedouin culture introduced during the Hilalian migration was extremely conservative. Its persistence has been remarkable. It was to collide with the modern world during the Second World War and especially with the discovery of oil in the 1960s. It should be given at least a small place in the study of the root causes of Libya's modern dilemma.

In this chapter we can discern two seeds which were to germinate in the modern state of Libya under Gaddafi. The first is the coming of Islam and the second is the arrival of Arabs. The processes of Islamisation and Arabisation are separate. Those who write about Gaddafi differ about whether tribalism or religion has exerted the most influence on him. Since one of the main factors of Gaddafi's government has been his personal charisma, the argument becomes important.

The first Arab invaders, who were soldiers, were motivated by their faith. Islam brings with it a powerful combination of faith, law and language. It is based on the Koran, the sacred book of Muslims, which contains the word of Allah received by and through the Prophet Muhammad. This is supported and supplemented by the Hadith, the carefully composed traditions or sayings of the Prophet. From these sources is derived Sharia law, which outweighs all other considerations of tribe or nationality. The Koran and the Hadith are in what we now call classical Arabic. I join with a number of observers in expressing an interest in the importance of language in the formation of personality.

In Libya, Islam was quickly embraced by the indigenous Berbers. The origin of the Berbers is not certain, which makes historians uneasy. They spoke and wrote their own language, which still persists in small pockets of Libya, notably in the Gebel Nefusa. Whatever the obscurity of their origins, they were readily converted to Islam and it spread amongst them rapidly. It was the Hilalian migration that brought the true Arabs to Libya. They absorbed or marginalised the Berbers, and the Arabic language commenced its domination of Libya. It is the Arab tribal customs imported from the Nejd that prevailed in Libya. In his *Green Book*, Gaddafi emphasised the importance of the tribe. He also emphasised the relationship between religion and society by stipulating that every nation should have a religion so that the social factor concurs with the religious factor to create harmony.

Both Islam and tribal customs affected Gaddafi profoundly. To these I add another factor. The geographical and cultural isolation of his early childhood and adolescence was exceptionally profound.

3

Ottomans and Turks
The Slave Trade, the Barbary Corsairs and the Four-Year War with the USA

By the end of the sixteenth century much of the Islamic world was under Ottoman Turkish domination. Tripoli fell to the corsair Dragut in 1551 and remained in Turkish hands, along with the rest of Libya, until 1911. Tripoli has always tended to be a city state and, though its influence and sometimes rule extended to other coastal towns, it was rarely able to dominate the interior.

During this period, Tripoli's strategic position, dominating the sea routes of the southern Mediterranean, enabled it to gain revenues from state piracy. It also brought it into focus when France, Britain, the USA and later Italy widened their strategic ambitions in the region.

The trans-Saharan trade, especially in slaves, brought revenue and eventual opprobrium. When it was diverted through West African ports, the trade in Libya fell off, though it persisted in a small way until 1930.

From its foundation in 1842, the Islamic Senussi Order grew rapidly to form a quasi-state. It was to play a decisive role in modern Libya.

The Ottoman Corsair Dragut Takes Tripoli

In 1959 I was visited in Tripoli by the British vice-consul. He brought along some old letters which he had saved when the ancient files of the Tripoli Embassy were being weeded. One letter instructed the Tripoli consul to ignore all instructions that might come directly from the king. I take this to mean 'Mad King George' and, thus, I am able to date the letters broadly, something I failed to do in my diaries. One letter from the government in London instructed the British consul to make a survey of the slaves sold by the Bey of Tripoli and the number that were castrated. There is clear evidence from the Tripoli records of this period that there was a trade through the port in slaves destined for the markets of the eastern Mediterranean.

According to Hugh Thomas, the North African slave trade continued after 1807, as it had throughout the era of the Atlantic trade. It had reached at least 8,000 slaves per annum by 1820. Included in those were a substantial minority of expensive eunuchs sought after as civil servants in the Muslim world of the nineteenth century.[1] Douglas Porch has surveyed a number of sources from the period, mostly eyewitness accounts by European explorers of the Sahara. He suggests that 5,000 slaves per annum were brought by caravans to Tripoli and that many failed to survive.[2]

E. W. Bovill, in *The Golden Trade of the Moors*, tells us that the Fezzan–Kawar road was an important route for slaving in the early nineteenth century because of the cordial relations that the Turks of Tripoli had established with the Sultan of Bornu. Reports by European explorers who travelled this route tell of human skeletons observed along the way, especially on the approach to water wells. Here the skeletons were mostly of women and young girls, showing how the effort to reach water only led to death from exhaustion.

From contemporary sources, Porch tells us that male slaves were usually chained together by the neck for the duration of the journey, whilst women and children were allowed to wander free. When the caravan arrived at one of the oases, slaves were sometimes sold to the oasis dwellers or to others who would fatten them for the Tripoli market. The British explorer Lyon wrote this of the market in Murzuk: '[The seller] runs from side to side of the street, crying in a shrill voice the price of the last bidder … the poor creature follows him at a trot, like a dog to the different groups of merchants who are sitting on the sand.'

The historian John Wright states that Benghazi had quietly continued as the last Mediterranean outlet for the trade almost until the Italians arrived in 1911. He goes on to state that there was a weekly slave market in the desert oasis town of Kufra until 1930.[3]

For all these reasons and more, the city state of Tripoli was an attractive prize. It is not surprising that the Ottomans coveted it. In 1510, the forces of King Ferdinand of Spain destroyed Tripoli and built a fortified naval base from the rubble. Ferdinand ceded it to the sometime crusader order of the Knights Hospitaller, but their occupation of the fortress was insecure and they were summarily ejected by the corsair Dragut in 1551. The corsairs were unable to hold Tripoli with their limited resources, so they ceded it to the Sultan of Turkey and it was, thus, absorbed into the Ottoman Empire.

The Ottomans extended their rule southwards from Tripoli and, by 1580, the chiefs of the Fezzan finally became their allies, thus ensuring the trans-Saharan slave trade for the Tripoli merchants. Tripoli was to remain, though sometimes nominally, a Turkish province for the next 300 years.

Dragut was made an admiral in the Ottoman navy. He was born in Anatolia of Greek parents and went to sea at the age of 12. He was a talented soldier and sailor and rose to become a protégé of Hayrettin, one of the famous Barbarossa brothers. He was a corsair, a privateer operating with a letter of marque from the Ottoman sultan. Like Oruch Barbarossa, he too was captured and enslaved by Christians, an experience that strengthened his commitment to piracy in the name of Islam. Dragut was an ambitious and ruthless man and, after he and Sinan captured Tripoli from the Knights Hospitaller, was appointed Sanjak Bey of the province of Tripolitania in August 1551.

Dragut was killed on Saturday 23 June 1565, in the great battle between the Ottomans and the Hospitallers of St John in Malta. His body was shipped to Tripoli and buried in the Dragut mosque situated behind the castle. The mosque is still in use today.

Ottoman rule was exercised by governors or pashas appointed by the sultan in Constantinople. They had full powers to rule, providing they remitted an annual sum to the Ottoman treasury and obeyed the sultan's commands. They were assisted in their rule by a diwan or council of local notables, a civil secretariat and Ottoman military officers known as aghas. The latter were in command of the janissaries.

The janissaries were Ottoman troops stationed in the pasha's province. By the seventeenth century they were recruited from the streets of Constantinople and the Levantine sea ports. They were exempt from taxation and from any work other than their military duties. They were required to live in their barracks, were forbidden to marry and subject only to military law. The enforced idleness of their life and their less than desirable origins made them the bane of the local civilian population. They were, of course, prone to stir up trouble and their aghas were not averse to intrigue.

The long course of Ottoman rule in Triopli was interrupted by an extraordinary interlude when a local dynasty seized power and exercised it, nominally on behalf of the Ottoman sultan, for a century and a quarter. The dynasty was in power when the first war between the USA and Libya occurred. We can say with confidence that Libya was then a pariah state, not for the last time. The first war with the USA is still a legend in modern Libya and in the USA.

The first native of Libya to rule Triopli was Ahmed Karamanli. He emerges into history in 1711. Tradition has it that the Karamanli family was founded by a corsair from Caramania, who came to Tripoli with Dragut, married locally and settled in the menshia, that is the cultivated oasis which surrounded the walled city. The tradition, as ever, may be a dramatised version of the truth.

The first Karamanli to seize power in Tripoli was the commanding officer of the Tripoli version of the famous Ottoman 'feudal' cavalry, known as the Kuloghlis. The name, incidentally, is derived from the Turkish *kul-oghli*, meaning son of slaves. Kuloghli service bore some similarities to feudal knighthood.

Ottoman provincial governors were supported by janissaries, who were foot soldiers. A cavalry arm was essential. This was especially so in Tripoli, where it was needed to keep the caravan routes open and the desert tribes in check.

During the expansionist stage of their empire, the Ottoman Turks had plenty of conquered land available. This allowed them to make land and tax concessions to their cavalrymen in return for military service. Thus a military cast of cavalry leaders grew, attached to the land and giving armed service in return.[4]

The Kuloghlis became assimilated into the population, but retained their obligations, rights and privileges. In Tripoli they had farms and businesses. Naturally they excited the jealousy of the janissary commanders and were not allowed through the town gates without permission.

In 1711 the official Ottman governor of Tripoli was Khalil Pasha. His rule was shaky and he was opposed by the janissary aghas. Eventually one of them, Mahmoud Dey, unseated him and turned his attention to the subjugation of the Kuloghlis commanded by the popular Ahmed Karamanli. It was an error. Ahmed Karamanli, leading a horde of Berbers and the local Kuloghlis, marched into the city and became the Bashaw of Tripoli, Misurata, Benghazi, Derna and Murzuk and nominal overlord of the tribes in the interior.

He and his descendants ruled their regency from 1711 to 1835. We have an eyewitness account of Ahmed's grandson, Mohamed Karamanli, as he rode in state through the streets of Tripoli. It comes from the letters of Miss Tully:

> The Bashaw, the Bey, and his second son, Sidy Hamet, went today to attend the mosque. None but the royal family ride in town. Their suit is followed on foot, excepting the head Chaoux, who is first in the possession, richly drest and mounted on a stately horse: he has a large kettle-drum before him on which he strikes minute strokes, going before in the manner of herald, proclaiming the Bashaw at the beginning of each street ... The insignia of the tails were carried next (The sovereign of Tripoli being a Bashaw with three tails): then followed ten hampers, or the Bashaw's body-guard, very richly drest, who carried short silver sticks in their hands ... The horses of the Bashaw and Bey were particularly beautiful and were buried in their trappings. Both their saddles were embossed in gold, and the golden stirrups weighing more than thirteen pounds each pair. The Bashaw's horse had on five solid gold necklaces; the Bey's horse three. The Bey wore a pale green and silver caftan, and a crimson shawl with rich gold ends twisted over his turban ... You may perceive that in few places the costume can be grander than it is here.[5]

There were two slave markets in Tripoli, one behind the Karamanli mosque for the Christian slaves brought in by the corsair fleet and the other for the African slaves brought across the Saharan caravan routes. There were two main routes that terminated in Tripoli. One began in Bornu and went to Tripoli via Kawar and the Fezzan. The other began in Kano and went to Tripoli via Air, Ghat and Ghadames. A third route was from the Wadai to Benghazi via the oasis of Kufra. The northbound trade was in slaves, ivory and gold dust. Southbound, the caravans carried cloth, beads, gun flints and gunpowder.

The three principal oases of Tripolitania and the Fezzan were Ghadames, Murzuk and Ghat. When the slave trade was at its height the oases were flourishing and green. They were also veritable towers of Babel. As well as Arabic, it was common to hear Tamahaq spoken by blue-veiled Tuareg and the languages of West Africa. Nomadic Arabs and Tuareg often camped on the fringes of Ghadames and demanded food and goods from the residents. Most of the work in the oases was done by the Haratin. These were serfs, in effect, and generally lived in mud huts in the gardens and palm plantations.

Professor Donald R. Wright has suggested that:

> Over the course of more than a thousand years, the trans-Saharan slave trade saw the movement of at least 10 million enslaved men, women, and children from West and East Africa to North Africa, the Middle East, and India. The slaves and their descendants contributed to the harems, royal households, and armies of the Arab, Turkish, and Persian rulers in those regions.[6]

The city state of Tripoli was for many years a nest of corsairs. By maintaining a small navy of shallow-draft vessels, often manned by Christian renegades, the rulers of Tripoli were able to pursue a lucrative trade in state-sponsored piracy. Tripoli, Tunis and Algiers were together known as the Barbary States. History is not without complaints about the Barbary pirates, their deprivations around the Mediterranean shores and their preying on merchant vessels. Tripoli was the lesser of the three Barbary States, with the smallest corsair fleet.

There is some value in comparing the Barbary corsairs to the Somali pirates of the early twenty-first century. They have proved how easy it is for small, fast motorboats manned by ruthless crews to capture unarmed merchant vessels in the

Indian Ocean. The Somali pirates hold crews and ships for ransom and have set up an autonomous state called Puntland.

The Tripoli bashaws were well rewarded with ransom money for wealthy captives. Failing that, some of their captives were sold into slavery, women being in high demand. However, the major maritime states were ready to pay good money to exempt their shipping and captives from the attentions of the corsairs. Britain, France and other leading maritime states signed treaties with the Bashaw of Tripoli and accredited consuls to him to see that their ships and citizens were safe. The threat of piracy was profitable.

War with the USA

The state-sponsored piracy led to a famous war with the USA. When the thirteen colonies in America made their declaration of independence, they lost the protection of the Royal Navy. American merchants sent their ships out into the oceans to find as much trade as they could. Those of their ships which ventured into the Mediterranean were harassed by the Barbary pirates from the pariah states of Algiers, Tunis and Tripoli.

So bad were the depredations that in 1794 the US Congress authorised the construction of a navy to defend American trade. An American consul, Cathcart, was stationed in Tripoli and, via him, the US offered the bashaw an annual payment of $18,000, plus a present of $4,000, to buy off the corsairs.

The bashaw, Yusuf Karamanli, was sure that the fledgling US navy was too weak to attack Tripoli and, therefore, decided to provoke the US Congress into making a more generous settlement.

He demanded a yearly subsidy of $250,000 and an immediate present of $25,000. As Cathcart was unable to pay, Karamanli chopped down the flagpole at the American consulate. This amounted to a declaration of war, so Cathcart left Tripoli. Karamanli's confidence that the Americans would avoid war and offer him a larger bribe was misplaced.

The US president, Thomas Jefferson, was under some pressure to limit aggressive intervention. The counter-pressure to deal with the Barbary corsairs, however, was impossible to ignore. He dispatched a small navy squadron commanded by Commodore Richard Dale with limiting rules of engagement. Commodore Dale was ordered to cruise about in view of the Barbary powers and not to engage the corsairs unless they were seen attacking a US ship. He accomplished very little and returned to the USA.

Dale did have one success when his schooner *Enterprise* captured a Tripoli corsair off Malta, stripped it of its guns and ammunition, and sent it back with its dead and wounded to Tripoli. Karamanli made its captain ride around Tripoli town on an ass whilst wearing sheep's entrails around his neck.

In 1802 the US Congress, which had by now recognised a state of war between the USA and Tripoli, dispatched Commodore Richard Morris to the Barbary Coast with a squadron and slightly more belligerent rules of engagement. Morris failed to show an aggressive spirit; perhaps because he had Mrs Morris along with him. He did attempt to negotiate with Karamanli but was unable to reach an agreement. He returned home to be court-martialled and dismissed from the service.

There is no doubt that Dale and Morris might have been more warlike if they had not been severely hampered by their orders from Jefferson and if they had been properly equipped for the job. The vessels under their command were not suitable for chasing the light, shallow-draft, oar-assisted corsair boats, which made for the shallows when the US navy appeared.

In 1803, the US sent a third squadron to the Barbary Coast. It was commanded by Commodore Edward Preble, who had the frigates *Constitution* and *Philadelphia*, the brigs *Siren* and *Argus*, and the schooners *Enterprise*, *Vixen* and *Nautilus* at his disposal. He was authorised to charter more ships locally if they were necessary and available.

His rules of engagement were similar to those of his predecessors, but with some of the vessels at his disposal he could run inshore in pursuit of corsairs. However, he was operating during the autumnal gales, which tend to drive sailing ships on to a lea shore.

Preble ordered the frigate *Philadelphia*, commanded by Captain Bainbridge, to take up station off Tripoli and maintain a blockade. The *Philadelphia* was accompanied by the schooner *Vixen* for inshore action. The gales made it impossible for *Vixen* to maintain her station, so Bainbridge sent her off to patrol around Cape Bon.

Toward the end of October, Bainbridge spotted a number of Tripoli corsairs running for shelter from the gales. On 31 October, he engaged a corsair in the approaches to Tripoli harbour. He had men taking soundings and lookouts posted, but he was caught out by the treacherous Kaliusa reef which rises abruptly from the sea bed. The forty-four-gun *Philadelphia* hit it at speed with a following wind, and she was stuck fast.

Karamanli's renegade Scottish admiral, Peter Lyle, saw his chance and sent his corsair fleet out to pound away at the *Philadelphia*'s rigging. With his guns unable to reply, Bainbridge called a meeting of his officers and decided to surrender. For this, he has been roundly criticised.

The Tripolitanian boats ran alongside and the *Philadelphia* was boarded and her crew captured. They were landed below the castle at 10 p.m., and were paraded through the city in their undergarments. The officers were imprisoned in the town, but the crewmen were thrown into the notorious dungeons below Tripoli's castle. The 308 crew members of the *Philadelphia* were to remain in captivity for a long time.

When the tide turned, the *Philadelphia* was freed from the Kaliusa reef by Peter Lyle with a salvage crew. She was towed into Tripoli harbour and remained there as an embarrassment to the US navy. She also posed a threat to the balance of sea power in the Mediterranean, should she be restored and manned by Karamanli's navy. This and the incarceration of 308 of her sailors ensured that the USA would have to attempt to destroy the *Philadelphia* and free the sailors.

In the events that followed there were legendry feats of heroism performed by American sailors and marines. The great courage shown here was, thus, more important to the history and fighting spirit of the US navy and US marine corps than to the eventual release of the 308 prisoners.

Commodore Preble decided to destroy the *Philadelphia*. To do this he had to get a crew into Karamanli's well-defended inner harbour, destroy the ship and escape. He needed good information about the harbour defences, the disposition of the Tripolitanian navy and the winds and tides in the harbour.

Much of this he obtained from the prisoner Bainbridge and his officers who, strangely, were permitted to correspond with friends in the US fleet.

Lieutenant Stephen Decatur, USN, volunteered to lead the raid. For this purpose he was given a captured Tripolitanian ketch, the *Mastico*, renamed the *Intrepid*, and the brig *Siren*. Decatur and his crew trained rigorously and on 16 January 1805, after many difficulties, they began their attack. They disguised their ships as merchant vessels from Malta, but the *Intrepid* was loaded with explosives and fire-making material.

At night they brought the *Intrepid* alongside the *Philadelphia*, which they boarded, and quickly overcame the watch crew, laid their explosives and combustibles, and lit the fuses. They re-joined the *Intrepid*, but the alarm had been raised. They made their escape through a heavy artillery bombardment, but reached the harbour entrance.

As they left the harbour, the *Philadelphia* exploded and burst into flames that lit up the castle and the ships in the harbour. Decatur and his crew escaped aboard the *Intrepid* and the *Siren* to Syracuse in Sicily, to the admiration of their countrymen.

The march of William Eaton is now legend in the USA. It was extraordinary. Eaton was an old soldier who was the American consul in Tunis and an Arabic speaker. He had a plan to deal with Karamanli. This amounted to regime change, not unusual in modern times but this was an early example.

He planned to replace Yusuf Karamanli with his elder brother, Hamet, whom Yusuf had deposed in 1797 and exiled to Egypt. To do so, he proposed to land a large force of US marines on the coast, to be joined by Hamet Karamanli with an army funded by Washington. In fact, Eaton was given $1,000 and a small detachment of US marines led by Lieutenant Presley N. O'Bannon.

Eaton persuaded Hamet Karamanli to sign a treaty, in which he agreed to favour the US in return for Eaton's help in deposing Yusuf. In Egypt, they jointly recruited a number of mercenaries; two Arab bands of Bedouin and a guard of seventy men for Hamet. Eaton's original plan was to transport the claimant and his small army by sea in US navy ships, but Hamet Karamanli insisted on taking the land route. Eaton and his marines were happily ignorant of the difficulties they were to face.

On 15 March 1805 they set off on a march through the Western Desert of Egypt, the Marmarica and Gebel Akhdar in Libya until they reached the port of Derna. They had been resupplied at the Gulf of Bomba by the USS *Argus* on 15 April, but only just in time. Lt O'Bannon and his small squad of marines were hard pressed to keep the Arab irregulars and the mercenaries in line.

With this strange crew, Eaton made an attack on Derna, which was occupied by Yusuf Karamanli's governor and 800 troops with some artillery. Eaton, supported by the USS *Nautilus*, *Argus* and *Hornet*, took the town on 27 April 1805.

On 8 May, Yusuf Karamali's troops arrived from Tripoli, some 750 miles away to the west. They took up a position overlooking the town, with Eaton and his force now besieged in Derna. With the aid of the offshore guns of the three US navy ships he held the town tenaciously until news reached him that peace had been made in Tripoli between the US and Yusuf Karamanli. In fact, the US paid Yusuf Karamanli $60,000 to purchase the peace. Eaton's war was over, and Hamet Karamanli was left in the lurch to creep off back to exile in Egypt.[7]

By 1835, the Karamanli dynasty, like the slave trade, was in severe decline. The Ottoman sultan sent troops to Tripoli to exile the last of them, Ali II, and reclaim the province for the Sublime Porte.

Ottoman Decline and the Rise of the Senussi Order

As the Ottman Empire began to wear out, its officials in Libya became more lethargic. Tripolitania and Cyrenaica were separated in 1879, with the latter becoming a sanjak directly dependent on Istanbul. The local Turkish officials were happy to stay in town and leave the interior to its own devices, providing the tax revenues were maintained. They were thus uneasy but not overly so when a new religious order emerged in Cyrenaica.

During the Ottoman period, the Sufi Senussi Order was established in Libya. In 1842, the Algerian-born Islamic scholar and missionary Sayyid Muhammad ibn 'Ali Senussi found himself, by chance, taking up residence in Cyrenaica, near the ruins of the ancient Greek city of Cyrene. There he found, living amongst the native Bedouin, a number of holy men known as the Marabtin b'il Baraka. Like them, Sayyid Muhammad was an Arabic-speaking Sunni Muslim, familiar with Bedouin life.

There was also a flourishing cult of saints, the Marabtin, in Cyrenaica and tribes adjusted their annual migration to spend regular periods near the tomb of their patron saint. These tombs are often small, white, square structures topped by a dome. In my day, one such could be seen from the road from Benghazi to Benina airport, with the tents of a visiting section of the Awaqir tribe pitched nearby.

Therefore, the Bedouin found nothing unusual when, in 1843, Sayyid Muhammad, known as the Grand Senussi, and his disciples founded a Senussi lodge at al Zawia al Baida on the central Cyrenaican plateau. The new lodge was situated at a point where the territories of three important tribes met. Probably the best way to describe a Senussi lodge is an Islamic seminary and community centre. It was made up of a mosque, classrooms, storerooms and living quarters for the head and for the brothers of the order. Senussi lodges were self-sufficient and needed land and water to support the residents and their visitors. In order to attract a lodge into their territory, local tribes had to give up some of their productive wells and arable land to support it. It was thus an important step because good land and reliable wells were precious resources in Cyrenaica and not often surplus to requirements.

This is how it worked in practice. When a few tribes applied for a lodge, they received a visit from a member of the Senussi family. Important visitors were always entertained to a feast and displays of wealth. By observing the interplay of person-alities and their relative wealth, the Senussi visitor was able to spot the paramount sheikh and areas of surplus wealth. They then set up their lodge under his protection and it was he who negotiated their title to arable land and grazing rights. The lodge was then constructed where there was sufficient surplus acreage and water and was protected by the most powerful sheikh amongst the tribes.

The Grand Senussi moved from Baida to Azziyat and thence to Jaghbub, in the desert southwards of Tobruk. From here he allied himself with the Zuwayya tribe, whose home is the oasis of Kufra still further to the south. The Zuwayya traded across the desert as far south as Chad, Wadai, Darfur and Kano, and as far north as Ajadabia. The Grand Senussi's followers travelled with the Zuwayya trading caravans to establish their missionary lodges.

In the late nineteenth century, the time was ripe for a new burst of missionary energy and the Grand Senussi was so successful that, within his lifetime, a vast theocratic empire was established. It was a missionary empire which stretched westwards into Tripolitania, eastwards into Saudi Arabia and the Western Desert of Egypt, and southwards into the oasis towns of the Sahara.

Islamic orders are a way of life. One of the better known is the Wahhabi of Saudi Arabia, but there are many others. Their aim is to achieve a complete identification with god by means of contemplation, charity, living apart from the everyday world and performing religious exercises. For the Senussi Order, this was achieved by the contemplation of the Prophet Muhammad. Followers were urged to imitate Muhammad's life until he became their sole guide and counsellor.

Islam is a Bedouin faith at heart. It is easy to see that what the Prophet Muhammad taught the Bedouin of Saudi Arabia in the seventh century was well suited to the Bedouin of Cyrenaica, who still led much the same lives in the nineteenth and twentieth centuries. Its clear and simple principles, to do good, avoid evil and pray regularly, were appealing to a tough nomadic and semi-nomadic people who lived in tents and followed their flocks in a quest for water and grazing.

The Senussi Order was a success because, as the great anthropologist E.E. Evans-Pritchard once wrote: '[the Bedouin] need was for some authority lying outside their segmental tribal system which could compose intertribal or intersectional disputes and bind the tribes and tribal sections within an organisation and under a common symbol.'[8]

It was also helpful that the Turkish occupiers of Libya were largely confined to the coastal towns and lacked the arms and will to destroy it.

Many years later, during the Italian occupation of Cyrenaica, the Senussi Order was given a new lease of life and became almost politicised. The Italians found it impossible to deal with the many powerful and independent tribal sheikhs. They found it easier, as did the British after the Second World War, to deal with the head of the order, Sayyid Idris, who was to become the king of an independent Libya in 1955.

The founder, Sayyid Muhammad (the Grand Senussi), created around him a group of disciples, the Ikwan, who lived the pure life of Islam. In Cyrenaica, only the Ikwan were able to recite the special prayers and follow the rituals. The Ikwan lived in lodges built within the tribal homelands and held prayer meetings there. The Ikwan were missionaries in the true sense of the word and they lived cheerfully and dressed well. They were self-supporting, growing their own food and herding their own animals. Thus, they avoided living on charity.

The ordinary unschooled Bedouin, Muntasabin, had little knowledge of the inner rituals and special prayers of the order, but they gave their personal loyalty to the sheikhs or leaders of the lodges in their territory.

The Cyrenaican Bedouin lived austere lives and thus many casual observers thought of the Senussi Order as being fanatical. It was not, but the drinking of alcohol was forbidden, as was the taking of snuff. In any case, these prohibitions existed throughout Islam and still do.

The Grand Senussi aimed to establish the conditions that would allow the Bedouin to live by their own laws and govern themselves, an aspiration which has recently plunged Libya into civil war. Apart from this, the Senussi were tolerant of Christians, Jews and other Muslims.

The Grand Senussi remained in Libya for only a few years before he moved on to establish lodges in Egypt and Arabia. His son, Sayyid Mohamed al Mahdi, who succeeded him, moved his headquarters to Kufra in 1895 and thence further south to Qiru in Chad in 1899.

The French, who were advancing their sphere of influence to Chad, were less than hospitable to the Senussi Order, so the Grand Senussi's third successor, Sayyid Ahmed al Sherif, moved his headquarters back to Kufra in order to retain control of the Wadai–Benghazi slave trade route. He was a

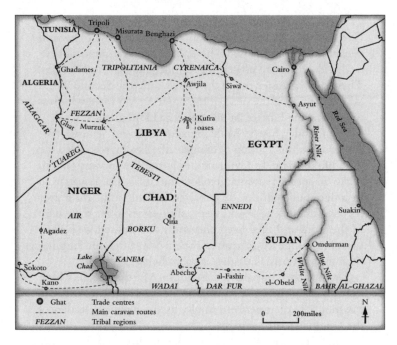

The caravan routes were used to bring slaves from sub-Saharan Africa
to the markets in Tripoli and Benghazi. The route from the Wadai to
Benghazi was said to be carrying slaves in the early twentieth century.

charismatic and inspiring Muslim and leader, who was both a
scholar and a soldier, leading the tribes in the First Senussi War.
He was defeated by the Italians and left Libya by submarine
in 1918. The Grand Senussi's fourth and final successor was
Sayyid Muhammad al Idris as-Senussi, who become King of
Libya when it became fully independent.

From this brief description of the foundation and spread
of the Senussi Order, it will be clear that it penetrated rapidly from its first foundation lodge near Baida, mainly via the
slave-trading routes from Kufra to the Sudan, Chad, Mali and
northern Nigeria. It was pushed out of the Sahel states by the
French. However, its firm hold on the nine Sa'adi tribes in
Cyrenaica was to give it a key role in modern Libya.

The Turks became embroiled in internal and international
difficulties and, in 1911, the way was open for the Italians, who
had coveted Libya for some years.

4

Italian Libya
The Battle for the Sword of Islam

The Italians colonised Libya from 1911 until 23 January 1943, when the British General Bernard Montgomery, at the head of the victorious 8th Army, entered the undefended city of Tripoli. For the Libyans this day marked the beginning of the end of a foreign occupation of notable brutality.

The Italian story of their invasion, occupation and colonisation of Ottoman Libya is for other historians to recount. A different perspective is needed here. Muammar Gaddafi made much of the stirrings of Libyan national leadership that emerged at this time. The guerrilla resistance by Libyan Arab tribesman, led by the Islamic teacher and soldier Omar Mukhtar, has been presented by him as the opening struggle for independence, which he was to complete.

In March 1937, Benito Mussolini was presented with the 'Sword of Islam' by Libyan notables in the great square before the ancient castle in Tripoli. It was the same square where Muammar Gaddafi was later to deliver long and unscripted orations.

There was a photograph made of Mussolini's presentation for the lavish magazine *Libya*. In it, Il Duce is caught obviously shouting whilst sitting astride a horse and resting the sword on his left shoulder. The old castle wall is in the background and Mussolini is flanked by two senior officers, also on horseback. One of them is the bearded Air Marshal Balbo. Standing before Il Duce, at the head of his horse, are two soldiers, each carrying large ceremonial fasces. The fascist symbolism is clear.

By receiving the Sword of Islam, the Christian Mussolini hoped to persuade the Muslim Libyans that he was the protector of their faith. The sword was made for him in Florence and it is unlikely that true Muslims, protected in any case by their caliph, would be fooled by such blatant propaganda.

The fasces, originally a bundle of rods surrounding an axe, were a symbol of authority emphasising continuity with imperial Rome. Mussolini intended to demonstrate that the ancient Roman Empire in Libya had been recovered by a new Caesar.

Power has a strange way with people. As a socialist agitator, Benito Mussolini had been imprisoned in 1911 for his opposition to the war with the Ottman Turks, which had established the first Italian imperial lodgement on the Libyan shore. His conversion to fascism had brought about a notable change in outlook.

During the same visit, Il Duce officially opened the new road, which stretched for 1,300 miles or so, from the Tunisian to the Egyptian border. It replaced the old pilgrim route taken by Muslims from Morocco, Algiers and Tunisia on their way to Mecca. It took three weeks for their camel caravans to travel from Tripoli to Derna. Now the new motor road had rest houses at intervals along the way and the journey by car could be accomplished in two days if necessary. Its construction had been funded by Italian tax payers and it had been built by Italian-supervised Libyan labour. Its true purpose was to facilitate the movement of Italian troops. It was officially known as the Via Litoranea. Unofficially it was called the Via Balbia.

Set in the wall of the Italian air force officers' mess at Castle Benito, the military airfield a few miles inland from Tripoli, were a set of sea blue ceramic tiles depicting a squadron of Savoia-Marchetti flying boats. The tiles celebrated the Atlantic crossing by a squadron of aircraft of the Regia Aeronautica led by Air Marshal Balbo. It was that same Balbo who was the Italian proconsul in Libya when Mussolini visited in 1937.

The Italian city of Tripoli had replaced the old Ottoman town. Its development began in 1922 and by 1937 it was lavishly supplied with civic splendours of the fascist genre. Flying boats linked Tripoli to Benghazi and Rome. A Grand Prix motor-racing stadium drew international crowds and notable racing aces. Tourists, accommodated in smart hotels, visited the ruins of Leptis Magna and Sabratha.

The Italian colony in Libya was at its zenith in 1937. How did it reach such commanding heights? The summary of the

Italian colonial adventure in Libya can give but a few glimpses of an otherwise complex history.

The Italians preceded the invasion by a protracted period of investment, trade and sporadic settlement. During this time the Banco di Roma, which led the commercial exploitation, had waged a propaganda campaign to promote its business. It had the effect of drawing both government and popular attention to Libya. The state of Italy, which was no more than 50 years old, was unstable, impoverished and leaking people at an alarming rate to the USA and South America. The attractions of Libya as a destination for Italian emigrants were advertised vigorously.

The Italians were drawn into the great imperial scramble for Africa led by the British and the French. Strategic considerations also focused Italian minds on Libya because it dominated navigation routes between the eastern and western Mediterranean and the land routes to East and Central Africa. Therefore, the Italian government decided to establish a colony in Ottoman Libya.

The general situation was thus. In Turkey, a group of young army officers and students, called the Young Turks, had commenced to seize power in 1908 and an effort to modernise the government was afoot. The effects of this had hardly penetrated as far afield as Libya. The Ottoman administrators of the Vilayat of Tripoli and the Mutasarrif of Benghazi were best described as pragmatic or, at worst, dilatory. Between them they were supposed to rule Tripolitania, the Fezzan and Cyrenaica. In effect, they ruled the towns and a few outposts. There were no roads outside the towns. As it had been since the Hilalian migration, the interior was ruled by tribal sheikhs who were not always in agreement with each other. To borrow a phrase, Libya was a Turco-Arab condominium.

The second part of Italy's colonial adventure commenced when she declared war on the Ottoman Turks. In 1911 she mounted an amphibious invasion of Libya, focused on the fertile coastal plain of Tripolitania and the city of Tripoli, where Libyan allies were easy to gain if not maintain. The Italians had achieved one of their strategic aims and now had control of the Mediterranean seaways between Sicily and Tripoli. To achieve control over the vast and hostile desert, they needed to acclimatise their army and develop the logistical, mechanical and military techniques of desert warfare. In addition, they needed to gain the support, or at least the neutrality, of tribal leaders who controlled the interior. It is worth reminding ourselves that this was a process which took the British and French some time to complete during the Second World War.

A number of writers have asserted that the Italians were unacceptably slow to follow up their capture of the five towns by pushing inland against the small Turkish forces, now some miles out in the hinterland. In doing so, these authors betray a lack of understanding of amphibious warfare. It was not until the US forces had perfected their amphibious warfare techniques in the Second World War (against the Japanese in the Pacific) that they were able to make the successful Torch Landings in North Africa and eventually succeed in the Normandy D-Day landings.

There is certainly some truth in the assertion that, in 1911, the Italians expected the capitulation of the local population to follow soon after their landings and were surprised by the resistance they encountered as they consolidated their bridgeheads and began to probe into the country.

The situation was complicated on 17 October 1912, with the Treaty of Lausanne between Italy and Turkey. The Italian people had been promised by their politicians that the invasion of Libya would be accomplished without undue loss of life. The Turks were about to embark on their war in the Balkans. The Italians were therefore ready to sign a treaty which gave the appearance of achieving their aims, but the Turks were more subtle. They could not be seen to surrender part of the Land of Islam (Dar al Islam) to a Christian power. What is more, the Turks wanted to encourage the Arabs to continue resisting the Italians in the name of the Sultan of Turkey, who was also the Caliph of Islam. The treaty allowed the Arabs to continue to recognise the Sultan of Turkey as their caliph, whilst the secular sovereignty of the King of Italy over Libya was affirmed. The sovereignty of Libya was thus divided between Italy and Turkey for some years.

From their lodgements on the coast, the Italians eventually turned their attention to the interior. In the meantime, the Turkish withdrawal from the Fezzan was spotted by the

French, who then advanced on it from their base in Algeria in 1913. The Italians were bound to react. In February 1914, they marched south through the desert to Sebha, the capital of Fezzan. However, the tribesmen in the Fezzan rose in arms, cut them off and harassed them as they tried to fight their way back to the coast.

The Italians now attempted to take the Sirtica, but the tribes, notably the Aulad bu Sief, soundly defeated them. As part of the Italian counter-attack in April 1915, the Italian Colonel Miani entered the Sirtica from Misurata with a 4,000-strong battle group. He was accompanied by 3,500 Libyans led by Ramadan al Shutawi, the wily warlord of Misurata.

Arab resistance to his advance, led by the Senussi Sayyid Saif al Din, was concentrated in the Sirtica. Sayyid Saif al Din had with him some of the Tripolitanian tribes, notably the Aulad bu Saif. The resident Sirtica tribes, the Aulad Suleiman, the Magharba and the Gaddadfa, were also in arms against the Italians.

Col Miani's sometime ally, Ramadan al Shutawi, turned against him and helped Saif al Din's tribal warriors to defeat the Italians at Qasr bu Hadi on 29 April 1915. As a result of this notable defeat, the Italians lost their own rifles and ammunition, plus a reserve of 5,000 rifles and millions of rounds of ammunition, several machine guns and artillery with plenty of shells, the entire convoy of food supplies and even their bank. The Arab victory at Qasr bu Hadi has passed into Libyan tribal folklore and is passed from generation to generation. There was also a significant flowering of Berber independence, led by the notable personage Suleiman al Baruni in the Gebel Nefusa until it was extinguished for a while by the Italians in March 1913, at which time al Baruni fled to Turkey to return later.

The Italian defeat at Qasr bu Hadi was so decisive that they now withdrew from the country to the coastal towns.

The Great War diverted Italian attention from their colonial ambitions for some time. During this period the Libyans began to find some political unanimity. This resulted in a period when the Italians effectively ceded the interior of the country to an Arab Tripolitanian republic and the Cyrenaican Senussi Order.

The third phase can be labelled the Italian re-conquest of Libya – *La Reconquista*. We will take it in two parts, the first being the Italian pacification of Tripolitania and the Fezzan. The pacification of Cyrenaica is treated in more detail later in this chapter.

The Italian pacification of Tripolitania has been overshadowed by the publicity given to the Second Senussi War in Cyrenaica. It was also more complicated because the tribes were less able to co-operate. The details of the various engagements are difficult to compress. There is an overall pattern and, as is often the case, some personalities stand out as being influential.

At first the Italians were hampered by political instability at home and the consequent reluctance of the government to spend money or political capital on a colonial war. There was also some sympathy for the Libyans amongst the left-wing parties.

The appointment of Count Giuseppe Volpi in August 1921 as the eleventh governor of Tripolitania in ten years brought a character with ability into play. He gathered a coterie of effective army officers around him.

Benito Mussolini's march on Rome changed the nature of Italian colonial policy. From vacillation it shifted into ruthless decisiveness, and from occupation to expansion and agricultural settlement.

In Tripolitania the political situation was slow to resolve. The characteristic reluctance of Sayyid Idris to accept the emirate played into Italian hands and gave them time to mount a decisive amphibious landing to recapture Misurata marina in January 1922. This stiffened the Italian government's resolve.

The Italian army was generally better at logistics than combat, a handicap that was to emerge again in the Second World War. The Italians had aircraft at their disposal, which they used effectively, but there are persistent rumours that they dropped poison gas bombs and live rebels from their aircraft on to recalcitrant tribal camps. The first is more likely to be true than the second.

When politics in Tripolitania fail, the tribes emerge as centres of power. This has the effect of dividing power because the tribes are often in disagreement. However, by 1922 the Italians had attempted to occupy the whole of Libya. The primary opposition was centred in the remote Gebel Akhdar in Cyrenaica. This was the period of the Second Senussi War.

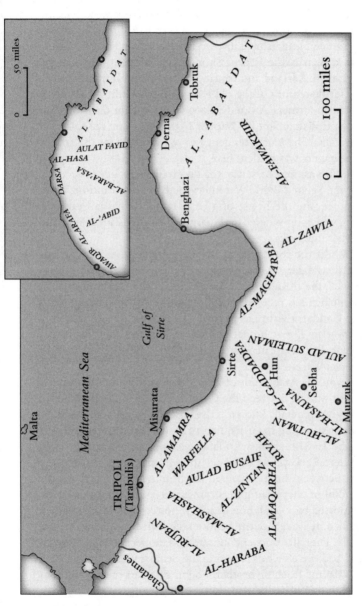

Some of the tribes of Libya as they were at the time of the Italian occupation (after Canivari and De Agostini).

The fourth period was one of demographic colonisation under the leadership of Air Marshal Italio Balbo, who became governor of both Tripolitania and Cyrenaica in 1934. Under his forceful leadership, Libya became an integral part of Italy. It was known as 'the Fourth Shore' when added to those of the Terranian, Adriatic and Ionian coasts. Balbo planned to settle the fertile regions of the old Roman Libya with vast numbers of Italian farmers. Around 10,000 were brought over together in the first shipment in October 1938. They were the so-called *ventimillia*. The Italian tendency to overestimate for the sake of appearances was evident here.

Balbo aspired to settle 500,000 Italians in Libya by 1950, but the Second World War intervened. In the meantime, Libya had become the home of a large Italian Christian population, which dominated and marginalised the Islamic Arab and Berber indigenes.

Whilst the resistance to Italian occupation in Tripolitania and the Fezzan was important, and the battle of Qasr bu Hadi crucial, the main centre of resistance in the Gebel Akhdar in Cyrenaica has received more attention. It has been used by the Gaddafi regime as part of its propaganda and the film, *Lion of the Desert*, depicting the work of the guerrilla leader Omar Mukhtar, makes further discussion of the Second Senussi War necessary.

From the Arab point of view there were two distinct periods of warfare between the Cyrenaica Libyans and the Italians. They are generally known as the First and Second Senussi Wars. The first, lasting from 1911 to 1917, was led by a few officers of the Turkish army, who later became important figures in modern Turkey. The second, lasting from 1923 to 1932, was a war between the mechanised might of a modern army and a handful of guerrilla fighters carrying a few, often stolen, arms, supported by a small population of hostile Bedouin, organised and led by leaders of the Senussi sect. It had the characteristics of the guerrilla wars encountered by modern armies today. It also had the effect of elevating the Senussi Order from a missionary and teaching brotherhood into a quasi-state, which was later to dominate the Kingdom of Libya.

The emergence of the Senussi Order as a quasi-state was brought about by the pressure of a Christian invasion. It found itself drawing together the Sa'adi tribes and their clients, and it gave strategic coherence to the battle against the Italians. The Italian invasion showed that Islam is capable of unifying several national and tribal forces, in this case the Turks and the Libyan tribes, against a common threat. The modern state of Libya felt its first birth pangs during the two Senussi wars, which, therefore, need some attention from a Turkish and Arab perspective.

The First Senussi War

When the Italians commenced their Libyan adventure, Sayyid Ahmed al Sherif, residing in Kufra, was head of the Senussi Order. It was his decision to continue the war against the Italians. This brought his network of religious centres into focus as leaders of resistance. He instructed his representatives to raise the Arab tribes against the Christian invaders in the name of the caliph. This was an outcome the Italians had not foreseen and it had enormous consequences.

His representative in Benghazi, Sheikh Ahmad al Isawi, raised the local tribes to join the Turkish garrison, which had retreated from Benghazi to Benina, a village 12km east of the town. With these tribal irregulars, the Turks stopped the Italian advance into the interior.

The Turkish garrison at Derna had also retreated to a position behind the town, and were there joined by tribal warriors from eastern Cyrenaica who had been roused by the Senussi representatives. A third Arab irregular force joined the Turkish garrison of Tobruk, which had similarly retreated into the hinterland. Thus the First Senussi War commenced when the Italians made their five-point amphibious assault on Libya in 1911. In the beginning it was a Turko-Arab war for which the Libyan tribes, led by the Senussi Amir Sayyid Ahmed al Sherif, supplied most of the manpower.

The Turkish point of view is less often heard. As soon as war with Italy broke out, the Ottoman war minister, Sevket Pasha, admitted that Turkey would not be able to defend her Libyan possessions because her army was too weak and her navy almost non-existent. Troops had already been moved from Tripoli to defend the Yemen.

However, the Young Turks decided to defend the indefensible. Their leading light, Major Enver, immediately left his post as military attaché in Berlin to persuade his colleagues to launch a guerrilla war against the Italians in Libya by mobilising the Arab tribes there. He and all other revolutionary officers of the Young Turks rushed to Libya by any means they could. They had no official cover from their government and, if they were caught, they were to be described as adventurers acting against the wishes of the Ottoman administration.

The Young Turks joined up with units of regular Ottoman troops still in Cyrenaica. Azziz al Masri, later to be the inspector general of the Turkish army, joined the Benghazi siege; Mustafa Kamal, later the first President of the Turkish Republic, and Enver, later Turkish Minster of War, joined the siege of Derna; and Adam Pasha al Haiabi joined the siege of Tobruk.

The Turko-Arab campaign pinned down the Italians in the coastal towns. It was characterised by the tension between the well-trained and experienced Turks and the undisciplined, adrenaline-fuelled wildness of the tribes they directed.

A regular submarine shuttle service between Turkey and the coast of the Gulf of Sirte ensured that the tribes and the Turks were supplied with arms, ammunition and funds. The little port of Misurata was often used for this purpose after the Italians foolishly abandoned it. It was to emerge into history again during the rebellion of 17 March 2011.

In April 1913, the Italian forces broke out of Benghazi, captured the Libyan camp at Benina and pushed on northeastwards into the Gebel Akhdar. A further force made an amphibious landing at Tolmayta and also advanced into the Gebel Akhdar as far as Barce. The combined force now pushed the Arabs back as far as Tobruk and the morale of the remaining Turkish forces was broken. They withdrew to Egypt, leaving the Arab tribesmen in the Gebel Akhdar to carry on the fight as guerrillas.[1]

Much blood was spilt in heroic skirmishes and the effect was to limit the Italians more than they had bargained for. In Cyrenaica, the Great War brought complications. Italy joined the war on the side of the entente powers and Turkey on the side of the central powers. The Italian war machine was now focused on Europe. Many of the Young Turks left Libya to join the major Turkish conflicts. However, enough remained and Sayyid Ahmed was dragged into a disastrous military adventure against the British in Egypt in 1915. The Turks were desirous of diverting British forces away from their efforts in Palestine.

This is what happened. The Turks persuaded Sayyid Ahmed to raise a Libyan Arab force with which he crossed into Egypt in November 1915 and, for a while, occupied part of the Western Desert. His force was defeated by the British in March 1916. It was the last straw, and caused Sayyid Ahmed, already conscious of the wartime deprivation of his people in Libya, to resign in favour of his cousin, Sayyid Idris.

Sayyid Idris had reached an understanding with the British in Egypt in 1916, which was to have a long-term influence on Libya. Sayyid Ahmed left Libya for good and the First Senussi War petered out in 1917. Sayyid Idris entered into a period of negotiations with the Italians, in which the British were to be involved as brokers.

The negotiations were complex, as were the intertribal wars and skirmishes. The fierce warrior Ramadan al Shutawi of Misurata played a notable part in events by throwing his weight around. For a while, a Tripolitanian republic existed. This was unwelcome to the Italians, who were still unable to break out of their base in Tripoli. Attempts to quell the republic involved the bombing of Misurata by British aircraft based in Malta.

In Cyrenaica the British were anxious to reach an agreement with the Senussi in the person of Sayyid Idris. Tripartite negotiations took place between the Italians, Sayyid Idris and a Colonel Talbot representing the British. The upshot was that Sayyid Idris was appointed Amir of Cyrenaica, with considerable autonomy over the oases in the interior. This appointment was written into the Accord of al Rajma, dated 25 October 1925. In return, Sayyid Idris agreed to call off his guerrilla bands in the Gebel Akhdar and renounce his interest in the Western Desert in Egypt. This meant that the British no longer had to station troops there. The British had gained, Sayyid Idris had gained, but the Italians had lost.

Sayyid Idris formally accepted the emirate and delegated his responsibilities in Tripolitania to a committee under its president, Ahmad al Marayid. He then fled the scene by camel caravan to the oasis of Jaghbub and thence to Egypt, where he had acquired property. This was his characteristic reaction to stressful situations. He left his brother Sayyid Mohamad al Rida and his cousin Sayyid Safi al Din in charge of Senussi business in Cyrenaica.

Sayyid Idris was not to return until the British held the reins of power in Cyrenaica. In 1944 his brief return was greeted by a public display of welcome, especially in the tribal strongholds, but he was wary of committing himself.

The Second Senussi War

Benito Mussolini had seized power in Italy in 1922 and his fascist regime was gaining power. It was only a matter of time before he projected that power into Libya. He did so and precipitated a war with the nine Sa'adi tribes and their clients, and with the great Senussi leader Omar Mukhtar. It was brutal and bloody. The tribes were defeated and decimated. Italians appropriated their land and brought in large numbers of settlers. It is claimed that nearly 50 per cent of the population of Cyrenaica perished during this period. The guerrilla war represents a historic struggle for independence in the minds of the Libyan people and Omar Mukhtar became Libya's first national hero.

US army officers serving in Afghanistan are encouraged to read *The Seven Pillars of Wisdom*, T.E. Lawrence's semi-fictional account of his exploits in the Great War during the Arab revolt. They do so to understand guerrilla warfare.

They might more profitably read the history of the Second Senussi War, about which Graziani, the Italian general who conducted it in the 1930s, wrote that the situation is 'like a poisoned organism which sets up at one point of the body, a poisoned bube. The bube in this case was the fighting band of Omar al Mukhtar, resulting from the entire infection ... the entire population took part in the rebellion.'[2]

When referring to the supply and sustenance of the guerrillas another author wrote that:

> ... the entire country was like a capillary system of roots which fed from their hidden depths the visible foliage of

the resistance. It was useless to try to destroy the plant of resistance by striking at its visible foliage, for when fighting the bands were hard pressed, they dispersed and resided amongst the sottomessi [the settled or subdued tribes] for rest, recuperation, and refitting.[3]

With aircraft in support, the Italians commenced hostilities in March 1923 with an attack by mechanised troops across the Barqa al Hamra (the Red Plain) and the Barqa al Baida (the White Plain), that is the western lands of the Awaqir and the homeland of the Magharba and Zuwayya tribes. Their objective was to seize Ajadabia.

They invested the town on 21 April. It was an easy victory over the ill-equipped Arab forces and the Italians expected their early capitulation.[4] They later detached two mechanised columns to attack Marsa Brega in the west, but they were severely mauled by Magharba tribesmen operating in their homeland. The Italians learnt quickly that disciplined columns of troops, moving in deliberate formation towards an objective, were vulnerable to harassing attacks by Bedouin bands fighting in their homeland with cover from dunes and rough country. I have driven over this country on frequent occasions and can confirm that it would be ideal fighting ground for the Magharba irregulars to raid and disconcert town-bred troops plodding through the sand.

The Italians were thwarted and adopted a new strategy. They took to sending out flying columns of mechanised troops to raid the Bedouin camps, killing men, women and children without mercy, destroying the grain stores and flocks, and then withdrawing quickly into their defended base in Ajadabia. These were terror raids designed to kill as many Bedouin as possible.

Some idea of the targets available to the Italians can be gained from this picture of the Bedouin camps drawn from Emrys Peters, who lived and worked amongst them in the 1950s:

The Zuwayya tribe occupy a triangular area with its apex at Ajadabia. In spring they are to be found about thirty miles to the south of the village ... In the summer they converge on the apex of the triangle. From April to November the camp of the Jululat section alone numbers over eighty tents, and a

mile away there is usually a huge camp consisting of more
tents. Practically the whole of the two largest sections of the
tribes ... pitch their tents within five miles of the village.[5]

In winter, when the camps were dispersed and the terrain
impassable, the Italians took to flying over them and machine-
gunning indiscriminately. Stories of the awful strafing raids
were still current when I was travelling through the Barqa.
The historical as well as the strategic significance of Ajadabia
is now clearly apparent. The way in which history is repeating
itself is disconcerting to say the least.

To view the subsequent events of the Second Senussi War
in detail is near impossible. A general description must suffice.
The Italians opened the Second Senussi War better equipped
than they were in the first. They had armoured vehicles and
aircraft at their disposal. It is estimated that by the end of 1926
they had 20,000 men in the field, mostly fanatically Christian
Eritreans. According to E.E. Evans-Pritchard, the best estimate
was that the Arab tribes could put 2,000 men in the field at
any one time, armed with modern rifles and a few machine
guns and artillery pieces. The same source states that there
were 3,000 to 4,000 rifles amongst the tribes.

Organised resistance by the tribes was impossible so they
pursued a classical guerrilla war, where sentries were shot,
supply columns ambushed and communications interrupted.
There was a succession of small actions and acts of sabotage in
different parts of the country.

At first the Italians responded by courting the favour of
those tribes, or parts of tribes, near the towns. By offering
employment, subsidies and arms, they hoped to turn them
against the rebels. In their minds there were two types of tribe:
the *sottomessi*, that is the submitted, and the *rebelli*.

They thought they had gained the loyalty of the *sottomessi*
to support them against the *rebelli*. They were to be constantly
disappointed. The *sottomessi* supplied arms, ammunition, food,
intelligence, shelter and funds to the *rebelli*. Sometimes the
tribal sheikhs would arrange amongst themselves who would
submit and who would take the field.

To their consternation, the Italians had overlooked or mis-
interpreted, as many do, the powerful Bedouin law. The nine

Sa'adi tribes and their clients were all Bedouin, jealous of each other and hostile to tribes other than their own. The males of each tribe were duty bound to avenge a slain kinsman. The group of males within the tribe who shoulder this collective responsibility is called the amara dam. The other side of this coin is the duty to protect and aid a living kinsman. This is at the root of Bedouin values. The common ancestry and the kinship of the Sa'adi tribes overrode the lesser demands. The tribes were united by blood, Islam and a common way of life against the Italians.

For the Western Arabist, or indeed anyone who works amongst the Libyans today, the most useful rule to follow is that which was enunciated by E.E. Evans-Prichard:

> ... the Bedouin mind is not all of one piece but a Joseph's coat of many conflicting interests. These interests exclude each other as the social situation evokes one loyalty to the detriment of another and it is therefore, only in terms of this social structure that the apparent inconsistencies of Bedouin behaviour can be understood.[6]

As the Italian proconsul Graziani wrote of the Second Senussi War: 'The entire population thus took part directly or indirectly in the rebellion.' However, the guerrilla war was led by some notable families who have received less attention than they deserve. They were the Abbar and the Kizzih of the Awaqir; the Saif al Nasr of the Aulad Suleiman; the Bu Baker bu Hadduth of the Bara'asa; the Lataiwish of the Magharba; the Abdalla of the Abaidat; the Asbali of the Arafa; the Suwaikir and the Ilwani of the Abid; and the Bu Khatara bu Halaiqua of the Hasa. The homelands of the tribes that these families led stretched from the desert south of the present city of Sirte to the Marmarica in the east around the city of Tobruk. All of this territory was ideal for guerrilla warfare.

The tribal leaders were formidable but they needed the co-ordinating hand of a leader. They found it in the person of Omar Mukhtar, who brought not only his considerable energy and talents into the field but also the network of Senussi lodges and intelligent personnel from throughout the tribal homelands.

In the Senussi Sheikh Omar Mukhtar they had a leader who, though he was over 60 years of age, was an experienced soldier and a talented tactician, with an almost unique ability to keep the peace between the fractious tribal detachments he commanded, perhaps because of his Bedouin birth. His parents were members of the Minifa tribe from the Marmarica. He planned all the operations, gathered and evaluated the intelligence, organised the logistics and finance, and led a guerrilla band of his own.

The Italians' response grew more heavy-handed as the war progressed. They found that the *sottomessi* were supplying the *rebelli*, so they commenced by disarming the non-combatant tribesmen. They went on to harsher methods to stop the flow of rebel volunteers, ammunition and weapons, money and food from the *sottomessi*. They used the well-tried methods of arrests, restricting civilian movements, deportations, aerial bombardment and strafing recalcitrant tribes. They blocked and poisoned desert wells, confiscated precious livestock and barbed wire was liberally strewn around to restrict the seasonal migrations. The rate of executions was alarming. John Wright quotes the traveller Holmboe, who was in Cyrenaica at this time, as stating: 'During the time I was in Cyrenaica thirty executions took place daily, which means that about twelve thousand Arabs were executed yearly ...'[7]

In the concentration camps, the *sottomessi* were seriously depleted in health, morale and numbers. One such camp is described by Holmboe thus:

> The camp was immense. It contained at least fifteen-hundred tents and had a population of six to eight hundred people. It was fenced in with barbed wire, and there were guards with machine guns at every entrance ... the Bedouins ... looked incredibly ragged. On their feet were hides tied with string; their burnooses were a patchwork of all kinds of multi-coloured pieces. Many of them seemed ill and wretched, limping along with crooked backs, or with arms and legs which were terribly deformed.[8]

They went after the Senussi lodges, destroying them and deporting their leaders. They captured Omar Mukhtar in

September 1931, when he was ambushed near Baida. He was wounded in the arm, while his horse was shot and pinned him to the ground, and he was taken prisoner. I have an old photograph from a magazine of Omar Mukhtar handcuffed to two Italians. He is wearing traditional Libyan dress and his beard is long. He looks formidable. Behind him is an Italian officer in white uniform, Graziani I am told.

The Italians tried Omar Mukhtar in a hurry. They made a spectacle of his final moments. He was hanged at a place called Suluq before an audience of 20,000 Libyans assembled there by the Italians. The rebellion was ended. A number of tribal leaders attempted to escape to Egypt.

The fourth stage of the Italian occupation was in full swing. Mussolini, as we have seen, was presented with the Sword of Islam. By 9 January 1939, the colony of Libya was incorporated into metropolitan Italy and thereafter considered an integral part of the Italian state. Libyans, then officially called Muslim Italians, were admitted to the National Fascist Party and Libyan military units were established within the Italian army. Two divisions of Libyan infantry participated in the desert war against Great Britain.

5

Second World War in Libya
The Desert Rats, the Desert Fox and the Free French

Muammar Gaddafi told Professor Edmond Jouve: 'We were under fire and dodging bullets in the middle of the Second World War. Countries were fighting over our land. We had no idea why. Planes were flying over our land. Bombs were falling. Mines were exploding all over the place. We did not know the reason why.'

From the point of view of Britain and the Commonwealth, this was the Western Desert campaign, which lasted from June 1940 to January 1943 and was fought to prevent Axis forces severing the Suez Canal, a vital Allied supply and communications artery.

For the Italians it was a debacle. They had declared war against the Allies on 10 June 1940 and moved their 10th Army into Egypt on 13 September 1940. They were beaten badly and so the Germans entered the field in March 1940, led by the notable General Erwin Rommel. He was aptly nicknamed the Desert Fox by the British.

His brilliant leadership nearly beat the British but Bernard Montgomery at the head of his 8th Army, the Desert Rats, drove him back from Alamein to Tripoli.

The Italians lost an empire. The Libyans, especially the Cyrenaicans, were free of them, but badly damaged.

Italy Goes to War

Everywhere I worked in Libya during the 1960s the Second World War had left its traces, discernable still after so many years. Out in the desert, initially out of range of British naval guns, the Italians had built their airfields. There the great doors of the aircraft hangers were still riddled with bullet holes. On

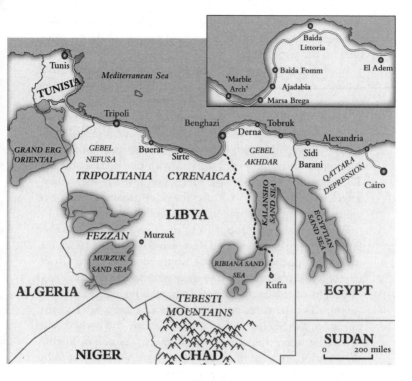

A map of Libya as it was during the Second World War campaigns. The
main physical features, such as the sand seas and the Gebels, are shown.
Note that the three provinces, Tripolitania, Cyrenaica and the Fezzan
are now known as Western, Eastern and Southern Libya respectively.

roadside walls were lugubrious cartoons, including a bald head
with a long nose peeping over a wall and the caption 'Kilroy
was here'. Passing motorists were, even then, cautioned by
signs which read: 'You will not laugh if Gerry strafes – keep
your head down.'

The Commonwealth War Graves Commission maintained
neat rows of gravestones in well-tended gardens, shaded by
eucalyptus trees. Whereas near Tobruk the German war graves
were huddled together up on a rise, within a Teutonic wall.

A number of small boulders, on which a skilled stonema-
son has carved regimental badges, lined the approach road to
Tobruk – neat and tidy and so very British. In a building some

few miles to the south of Tripoli was a fading mural depicting German soldiers at work; a rare and sad memorial to brave men on the wrong side.

In the 1960s, young American boys, at play in the Benghazi suburbs, dug up live ammunition and threw it onto bonfires to frighten adults – successfully. An unexploded mine acted as a step on which a shopkeeper stood to reach goods from a top shelf in his store near Tobruk. Great areas of Libya had been sown by both sides with anti-personnel and anti-tank mines, and people were stepping on them with nasty consequences. The landmine clearance companies employed reckless char-acters with strange CVs. Bailey bridges groaned under the increasing weight of traffic up in the Gebel Akhdar.

What was the war about from the Libyan point of view? From the perspective of the defeated and decimated tribes, the Italian colonial yoke was burdensome in the extreme. To be free of it and able to return to their traditional ways of living, to be rid of the Sicilians and Italians who were squatting on their best pastures, to revenge the butchery of Graziani, to restore the Senussi lodges and to destroy the barbed wire border between them and their fellow tribesmen in Egypt's Western Desert were things they may have wanted. Just to be rid of the Italians would be good enough to start with.

Many Libyan tribesmen who showed compassion and kindness to escaping British servicemen were punished by the Italians, sometimes by having their tents or houses destroyed and their families killed.

For Gaddafi, the point of view of his hero Nasser was cen-tral. As a boy Nasser would shake his fist at the British RAF biplanes flying over his home in Alexandria. The British fought their battle for Egypt and Libya for their own purposes. They were defending the Suez Canal and the route to their 'East of Suez' possessions. They stationed their considerable forces in Egypt and overrode its government when it had the temerity to assert some stirring of independence.

Hitler's Operation Eagle was lost by Goering's Luftwaffe in the famous Battle of Britain. Had it been successful it was to be followed by Operation Sea Lion, the amphibious inva-sion of England. Together they were to defeat the British, who were to become the subjects of the Third Reich.

Mussolini's attack on Egypt, from his base in Libya, was supposed to take advantage of the likely German defeat of the British and give him a stake in Egypt when the spoils of war were divided up. Mussolini was aware that the Italians could not hope to wage a major war because they were unprepared both militarily and industrially. His grandiose plan, as set out by him in the early stages of his dictatorship, was to achieve dominance over the Mediterranean by expanding westwards from Libya through French Tunisia, Algeria and Morocco. This was to be supplemented by expanding eastwards into the British sphere of interest in Egypt. Lacking the military might to achieve his ambitions, he decided to let the Germans do the work for him and to mark his ledger with an opportunistic invasion of Egypt. Once his troops were there he would be in a position to lay claim to Egypt if the Germans invaded and defeated Britain in Operation Sea Lion. He also made a thrust into British Somalia and expanded his interest in Abyssinia and Ethiopia with similar intentions.

It is notable that on 13 August 1940, Churchill wrote the following to the First Lord of the Admiralty:

> No one can see where and when the main attack on Egypt will develop. It seems however that if the Germans are frustrated in an invasion of Great Brittan or do not choose to attempt it they will have great need to press and aid the Italians to attack Egypt. The month of September must be regarded as critical in the extreme ...[1]

In the event, Fighter Command won the Battle of Britain, Operation Sea Lion was abandoned, Rommel brilliantly expanded German military might in Libya and Egypt, and Greece and Crete were captured by the Germans – with a little aid from Italy.

It was very brave, even foolhardy, of the Senussi amir, Sayyid Idris, to tie Libya's future to the British coat tails at that very dark time. No doubt he calculated that if the Axis forces won the war, Libya would remain an Italian colony, an outcome that was sufficiently undesirable to persuade many others to follow him. It won him the semblance of independence of his country in the end, but few would have predicted such an outcome.

At this stage a crucial event in the history of Libya occurred. It is often overlooked, even by the Libyans themselves. As the possibility of war with the British grew stronger, the Italians became uneasy about Sayyid Idris and a number of prominent Tripolitanian and Cyrenaican sheikhs living in exile in Egypt. They were afraid that the sheikhs would make their peace with the British with offers of assistance in Libya. They were right.

In October 1939, when it seemed certain that Italy would invade Egypt, the Libyan sheikhs met in Alexandria and formally recognised Sayyid Idris as their amir. They then informed the British ambassador that Sayyid Idris could speak for them in any future negotiations. Following Italy's declaration of war the sheikhs met again in Cairo on 9 August 1940 and decided to raise a Libyan force to fight alongside the British army in the Western Desert of Egypt.[2]

Consequently, the Libyan Arab Force was raised in Egypt early in the Second World War. It was recruited largely from Cyrenaican Bedouin who had fled the Italian atrocities perpetrated under the brutal Graziani or had been in the Italian army and had taken the first opportunity to surrender to the British. It was officered by British and Arabs, including some veterans of the Italian-Senussi wars.

There is no doubt that a large number of Libyans fought with the Italians against the British in the Second World War. This is something they prefer to forget, not without reason. However, it may be better to say that the Libyan army, as it is now constituted, germinated from the Libyan Arab Force. Some of the atrocities reported during the present civil war would have horrified many of its founder members.

One of its officers was a strange, very tough, Belgian émigré of Russian origin called Vladimir Peniakoff, known as 'Popski' by the British. Popski was a colourful, complex, not entirely truthful character, with a chequered past. During the First World War he was said to have been in Cambridge, where he was a pacifist. His sister, probably truthfully, stated that he was once enlisted in the French army as a chemist.

According to the military historian Julian Thompson, between 1924 and 1939 Popski worked for a sugar company in Egypt where he managed to wangle himself a commission in the Libyan Arab Force, becoming a company commander. Officers' commissions were issued in the name of the Amir of Cyrenaica, a de facto recognition of the style and title that Sayyid Idris had achieved. This was to strengthen the Senussi Order's claim to political leadership after the war and when independence was achieved. It also had considerable significance because the Aulad Ali tribe in the Western Desert region of Egypt was related to the Cyrenaican tribes, and we can be sure that news of the amir's new army would have leaked into Cyrenaica and Tripolitania.

The Libyan Arab Force had its own flag and badges but saw little active service, being used for garrison and guard duties, with one notable exception. In 1942 Popski was appointed to command a detachment of the LAF called the Libyan Arab Force Commando. Popski, with twenty-two LAF Bedouin soldiers and a British NCO, operated as an intelligence agent in the Gebel Akhdar and was regarded with respect, though more with fear than affection. Like him or not, Popski was the most famous Libyan Arab Force officer of the Second World War.[3]

It is said that Popski's effectiveness as an agent in the Gebel until the end of 1942 was notable. This was where a number of Axis airfields were in operation within range of the British in Egypt and the British needed to know as much as possible about them. His subsequent career as the commander of the independent and somewhat piratical Private Army, which operated in Tunis and Italy, was marred by a reputation for 'swanning' around looking for something to do. Popski, nonetheless, won a DSO and an MC for outstanding bravery during the Italian campaign.

Popski and his Libyans were amongst a number of British intelligence and sabotage units working within the tribes. Perhaps the most outstanding unit was the Special Air Service, which spawned the famous SAS of today. They were all helped by the British Long Range Desert Group (LRDG), which was one of the British independent units operating in the desert with the regular assistance of the Arab tribes. The Long Range Desert Group's main purpose was to keep a watch and report on the movements of Axis troops and supplies along the road from Tripoli to the Egyptian front. Its first forward base was the famous oasis of Siwa, the ancient seat of the oracle consulted by Alexander the Great. Siwa was an oasis with strong connections with the Senussi Order, and Sayyid Idris and his queen had escaped there from the less than tender treatment they would have received from the Italians.

Later the LRDG moved to Kufra to be better placed for its reconnaissance role behind Axis lines. Kufra was the centre of the Senussi Order for a long time. All this had considerable significance for Sayyid Idris.[4]

The Desert Fox and the 8th Army

The war in the Western Desert was a central event for the Libyans and is well enough known to need but a short summary here. In 1940 the Italian governor of Libya, the famous airman Marshal Balbo, was killed by his own anti-aircraft batteries whilst flying over Tobruk. At Mussolini's insistence his replacement, Marshal Graziani, moved the Italian troops at his deposal to the Libyan border with Egypt to threaten the British. In September 1940, he reluctantly moved his forces into Egypt but only got as far as Sidi Barani where, in December, his army was beaten decisively by the British Western Desert Force under General O'Connor. As a result, Graziani was driven back into Libya and was defeated again at Bardia and Tobruk. He was finally driven out of Cyrenaica in February 1941, at which point he pleaded a nervous breakdown and retired. Following this, the first British military government of Cyrenaica was set up, possibly under the command of Major General Duncan Cumming. Certainly E.E. Evans-Pritchard and other British Arabic-speaking officers commenced to make contact with the Bedouin tribes and lay the foundations for an independent Libya in the future.

Hitler only became involved when he sent a 'special blocking detachment' to assist Mussolini in defending Tripolitania. Rommel's arrival on 12 February 1941 accelerated the war somewhat, as it almost coincided with the withdrawal of a significant number of British troops for the ill-conceived Greek campaign. Rommel was given command of the embryonic Africa Corps and, ignoring an order by the German high command to remain on the defensive, launched a superb and bold attack which drove the weakened British out of Cyrenaica. Thus, the first British military government of Cyrenaica folded.

Rommel, leading a combined Italian-German army, went on to fight a fluctuating series of battles against the British over more than 2,000km of desert. These encounters were dominated by the struggle for sea and air control of the Mediterranean and the problems of supply of both the British and the Italian-German forces spread over hundreds of kilometres of desert, through inadequate ports and along a narrow coastal road originally built by the Italian colonists. That same problem of logistics and distance bedevilled the Gaddafi and rebel forces fighting in Libya in 2011.

In reality, Rommel's forces were numerically inferior to the British, but the latter took an inordinate amount of time to acclimatise and, until Montgomery took over, were unable to combine their infantry, armour and air arms to operate as a combined unit. Rommel also had a shorter supply line, at least whilst the Germans dominated the Mediterranean. In contrast, the British had to ship most of their stores 'around the Cape'. Rommel was also more daring than his British counterparts and the desert terrain gave him more room to manoeuvre his famous panzer tank units with consummate skill.

However, although he won a number of great victories, he did not have everything his own way. The Italians under his command were not as committed to the fight as he would have wished. Also the port of Tobruk, garrisoned by the British in the famous siege, always proved a tough nut for him to crack and so his eastward advances were dogged by supply problems.

During May and June 1941, he successfully repelled two British offences but was forced back in November by an attack codenamed Crusader. He received reinforcements and, emboldened by them, struck back in January 1942. By June he had captured Tobruk and had driven the British back into Egypt. He then became ill and without his leadership the German dominance diminished. The British held the line at Alamein, a desert halt on the main railway line from Alexandria to Mersah Matruh, and there they stuck. The rest is part of British popular history. Churchill flew out to Egypt, sacked Auchinleck and put new generals in his place. Bernard

Montgomery was now on the scene and he made thorough preparations for an offensive. He amalgamated the RAF head-quarters with his own, husbanded resources, trained his troops and briefed them thoroughly. When he was ready, he launched his attack. It was at 9.45 a.m. on 23 October 1942 when his opening 'shock and awe' barrage was heard as far away as Cairo. Twenty minutes later, his infantry attacked across the minefields, which had been meticulously cleared. The Battle of Alamein was joined. The battle lasted until the night of 3/4 November, when the British 1st Armoured Brigade broke through the Axis lines and the chase was on. This was the first victory won by the British against Axis forces in the war.

The 8th Army rattled though Cyrenaica and took the bomb-battered port of Benghazi on 19 November 1942. It met with German forces in a defensive position amongst the dunes at Marsa Brega. The dunes made it difficult for the tanks to manoeuvre but the British were not held up for long. Nor was it delayed much by the Africa Corps' determined stand at Buerat, 200 miles east of Triopli.

The 31st Highland Division and the 7th Armoured Division entered Triopli on 23 January 1943, to a delighted reception from the Arab inhabitants. The end of the Italian Empire in Libya was marked by the British, who raised the Union Jack at the flag pole on the castle walls.

The Free French in the Fezzan

After the war a French military administration was formed in the lightly populated region of the Fezzan. It was a coun-terpart to the British operation in Tripolitania and Cyrenaica. This was largely made possible by a little-known war that was waged by de Gaulle's Free French in the Fezzan. If only in the light of the French intervention on the anti-Gaddafi side in the 2011 civil war it warrants some explanation.

During the war in the Western Desert, the British, whose control over the Mediterranean was doubtful, were forced to send their ships carrying supplies around the Cape of Good Hope. This took time and occupied ships which were in short supply. Gaining air superiority over the Axis to suppress their

Stuka dive-bombers, harass their supply routes and attack their armour required a superior number of aircraft flown by experienced crews. The RAF method of supplying these aircraft was an example of dogged determination and ingenuity, which has sadly received less than its due recognition.

The aircraft were dismantled and shipped by sea from the UK to the port of Takoradi on the Gold Coast, now Ghana. There they were re-assembled and then flown by RAF air crews to Lagos and then to Kano within British Nigeria. From thence they were flown over a hazardous route to Fort Lamy in the French colony of Chad, which had declared for de Gaulle and the Free French. From Fort Lamy, the aircraft were flown to the Anglo-Egyptian Sudan, reaching Khartoum via el Fasher. The route now turned north to Wadi Halfar, Luxor and finally Cairo.

In 1941, de Gaulle had formed the view that the British could well be forced out of Egypt. He concluded that the Fezzan would be of pivotal importance in protecting the rest of French colonial Africa. At that time the French positions in Equatorial Africa consisted of Chad, the Middle Congo, Unbangi-Shari and Gabon. Chad's Guyanese governor was Félix Eboué, to whom de Gaulle sent an envoy of the old French aristocracy: Philippe, Comte de Hauteclocque, whose *nom de guerre* was Leclerc. Leclerc and others persuaded Eboué to declare Chad for the Free French, thus giving Leclerc a base from which to attack the Fezzan.

Leclerc was an interesting product of the French military system. He was trained as a cavalry officer in the French Military Academy at St Cyr and escaped the fall of France in 1940 to join de Gaulle's Free French in exile in London. He was promoted by de Gaulle to the rank of commandant (major) and sent to rally French Africa to support the Free French. This he largely succeed in doing, though he had some difficulty persuading the Gabon into the fold.

De Gaulle was anxious to invade the Fezzan to establish a foothold from which to defend French colonial possessions against the Axis. Fortunately, the British were also anxious to assist him so that their Takoradi air route was protected. It was thus that Leclerc, now a colonel, captured Kufra with some useful assistance from the British Long Range Desert Group.

As the French say, Leclerc had an army made of bric-a-brac but full of offensive spirit. Before the Free French and the LRDG attacked Kufra, Leclerc gave a speech designed as a call to arms. It was known as the oath of Kufra, in which he said: '*Jurez de ne déposer les armes que lorsque nos couleurs, nos belles couleurs flotterons sur la cathédrale de Strasbourg.*' This is best rendered into English as: 'We vow to fight on until we liberate Lorraine and our Free French flag flies above Strasbourg cathedral.' The oath becomes significant when we remember that the Free French had adopted the Cross of Lorraine as their symbol and it was superimposed on the Tricolour in their flag.

Leclerc discharged his oath with honour when he entered the city of Strasbourg in command of the 2nd French Armoured Division on 23 November 1944.[5] He and his small army captured Kufra in March 1941. By December 1942 he led 3,250 men and 1,000 vehicles to capture Murzuk. The Free French went on to capture Mizda and met up with the 8th Army in Tripoli on 26 January 1943, having covered 1,600 miles since leaving Chad. It was a feat of arms of which the French are rightly proud.

With British approval, more Free French forces moved north from Chad to take control of the Fezzan in January 1943. A French administration was formed, directed by a staff stationed in Sebha, but it was largely exercised by the family of Sayf al Nasir. This family is still prominent today.

The war moved on westwards after the Italians surrendered Tripoli to the British. The 8th Army, with Leclerc's Free French, removed the Germans from Tunisia and met the US forces moving eastwards from their successful amphibious landing, Operation Torch, in Algeria.

The military effort now focused on Sicily and Italy. Greece was still labouring under Italian occupation and Crete was a German stronghold. There was still much to do before other people's wars were over for the Libyans who were still, officially, living in an Italian colony – an anomaly which took some time to sort out.

United States Army Air Force in Libya

When the United States Army Air Force (USAAF) arrived in Libya, the airfields surrounding Benghazi were chosen as the base for Operation Tidal Wave, the low-level air raid on the Ploiesti oil refineries in Romania which supplied the Germans.

The Ploiesti refineries were beyond the range of bombers flying from Britain. The USAAF calculated that they might be reached from Benghazi by B-24 Liberator bombers fitted with extra fuel tanks.

Benghazi saw the arrival of a huge fleet of Liberators, along with all the ground equipment and personnel to support them. A model of the Ploiesti refineries was built in the desert over which the bombers practised their low-level bombing techniques.

The raid was launched on 1 August 1943, when 178 Liberators started up their engines, creating a huge dust storm in which one of them crashed. Of the 177 aircraft that left Benghazi for Romania, 53 failed to return and 55 suffered battle damage. Of the men who flew on the mission, 310 were killed, 108 were captured by the Axis and 78 were interned in Turkey. The raid damaged some refineries but they were soon back in production and, thus, Operation Tidal Wave was a heroic failure.[6]

In 1968, an RAF desert rescue team visited the well-preserved remains of a B-24 Liberator bomber found in the desert by geologists. It was the *Lady Be Good*. She had departed from Soluch air base in Libya on the afternoon of 4 April 1943 for a bombing mission on Naples, but turned back near the target because of sand in the engines. On her return flight, the crew made a navigational error and crash-landed 440 miles south in the desolate Kalansho sand sea in the Fezzan.

Eight of the nine crew members were eventually located in the vast waste and returned home to their final resting places. To this day USAAF Staff Sgt Vernon L. Moore's remains still await discovery.[7]

Aftermath of War in Libya

The Libyan point of view of the war is often drowned by heroic histories of the 8th Army, the Desert Air Force, the USAAF and the Free French. What we must do is attempt to see the aftermath in Libyan terms. The two good ports in Cyrenaica, Benghazi and Tobruk, were badly damaged. Benghazi had been bombed ruthlessly; Tobruk had been the victim of a notable siege and was devastated. Commercial life was almost extinguished but for the scrap-metal trade. There was work of a menial sort with the new occupying powers, the British army and the RAF, but little else. In Tripolitania many of the Italian colonists remained and civil life for them continued, but those small farmers who had settled in the Gebel Akhdar had been evacuated early in the war.

For the Bedouin in Cyrenaica, their old homelands were once again free and they reoccupied the Italian farms and returned to their seasonal migrations. They had no pressing need for plumbers, electricians or doctors. They chose their own leaders and needed no politicians, lawyers or bankers to manage their lives. The desert tribes of Tripolitania also returned to their traditional life, as did the Berbers in the Gebel Nefusa and the Tuaregs in their desert strongholds.

For the post-Second World War military and later civilian governments of the three provinces, there was a problem that nearly crippled the nascent Libya and which has left a debilitating legacy for those who seek to govern today. It should be a lesson that foreign governments which choose to intervene in the life of ordinary Libyans should note.

Italian rule in Libya was absolute. It was not concerned with managing the Libyan economy, but with the preservation of its own primacy. The Italians settlers were segregated from the local population, especially in economic matters. They failed to train Libyan artisans and administrators. No local middle class emerged and the urban Libyans were not integrated into the expanding colonial state. Therefore there was no viable elite to take over from the Italians at the end of the war. What is more, the urban Libyans failed to forge ties of patronage with the tribes. Thus the Italian colonial legacy gave

Libya shape but no viable state machinery capable of assuming the burden of government. The military government and its civilian successors had to create a state virtually from scratch.

In the short time available to them the best instrument they could find was the Senussi Amir of Cyrenaica, who headed a proselytising religious organisation. The Amir of Cyrenaica was elevated to King of Libya and became increasingly isolated and ruled through a diwan, or courtier government, with limited support. The courtiers were primarily concerned with their own preservation. In essence, the Senussi monarchy lacked strong economic and political institutions. It was, therefore, weak and fell quickly when challenged, to be replaced by another arbitrary government under Muammar Gaddafi, which was also largely engaged in preserving its own power.

6

Independence
A Child of the
United Nations

Despite losing the war, the Italians remained the lawful colonial power in Libya. At the Potsdam Conference in 1945, Britain, the USA and the USSR decided that the Italian colonies captured during the war would not be returned to her. What to do with Libya became a problem that was not solved until independence in 1951.

As the Great Powers wrangled about what to do, the Cold War began to dictate the outcome. To Britain, France and Italy, countries with an early interest in Libya, were now added the USA and the USSR. Unanimity was difficult to achieve between them. The Libyan people of the three provinces were of different minds about their aims. In the end they settled for a compromise because the alternatives on offer were undesirable. This meant that there was no sense of national identity in the newly independent Libya to catch the imagination of the people and drive them forward.

The United Nations Decides

The wrangling over Libya's post-war future began after the Battle of Alamein, when Anthony Eden, the British Foreign Secretary, made a statement in the British parliament to the effect that the Senussi of Cyrenaica would be forever free of their Italian colonial masters. This persuaded the Tripolitanians that the British intended to champion Senussi leadership of Cyrenaica and probably of themselves.

As early as 1942 the USA had floated four ideas about Libya's future. The first was that she should become an international trust territory under the auspices of Britain, France and Egypt. This proposal did not survive long. The British scuppered it because they still wanted the Cyrenaican airfields from whence to dominate the Mediterranean.

The second idea was to give Cyrenaica to Egypt and Tripolitania to Tunisia. This was unacceptable because the Italian population of Tripolitania would have diluted French control of Tunisia. More to the point, there was little confidence in the Egyptian government's competence.

The third idea was that Libya should be returned to Italy. This was quickly discarded.

The fourth idea was the creation of a Jewish settlement in the abandoned Italian farmsteads in the Gebel Akhdar in Cyrenaica. There was insufficient arable land in Cyrenaica to support the potential number of Jewish settlers and it was likely to have stirred up widespread Arab opposition. This was confirmed in late 1945 when a number of Libyan Jews were murdered during the pogrom of Tripoli, an event which was still recalled by witnesses working with my wife in the late 1950s and early 1960s.

By January 1943, Tripolitania and Cyrenaica were under British military governments. Resulting from their successful campaign there, the Fezzan was ruled by the French. By virtue of their geographical positions, the three provinces were becoming strategically interesting. It will be remembered that the range of military transport aircraft was limited in the mid-twentieth century and the Libyan airfields began to act as staging posts for air movements of freight and personnel. The airfields also became attractive to powers wishing to dominate the Mediterranean.

Cyrenaica was a potential base for British forces, as their hold on Egypt and Palestine had begun to weaken. As negotiations for Libyan independence proceeded, the possibility that Russia might covet Libya as a base in the Mediterranean concentrated Western minds.

France was loath to relinquish her bases in the Fezzan, since they guarded the remote south-west of her Algerian possessions and her colonial interests in the sub-Sahel territories, notably Chad. Gun-running routes from Egypt to rebels in Algeria became a growing concern for her. French traditional interests in the Sahara were a matter of national pride, which had been sorely tested during the Second World War. In reality, the dominant tribes were largely in control of the Fezzan and were in favour of a unified and independent Libya, though few people bothered to ask them. Fezzan, as usual, was the forgotten province. There were only 50,000 or so inhabitants and they were widely dispersed.

Tripolitania, more populated than the other two provinces and still with a substantial Italian presence, seemed to be in danger of a return to the status quo antebellum, a fate which was fervently opposed by the more sophisticated Arab politicians there. According to international law, Libya was still an Italian colonial possession. This remained the case until February 1947, when Italy signed a peace treaty in which her rights were officially renounced. However, she certainly moved to reassert them on behalf of the large Italian population of Tripolitania during the post-war negotiations. Fortunately for Libya, the so-called Four Powers forced her to relinquish her claim in 1948. The Italian threat had caused Arab sentiment in Tripolitania to move in favour of a unified Libya, despite misgivings about the possible dominance by the Senussi of Cyrenaica.

Military governments of territories captured in warfare were given legitimacy by the Hague Convention of 1906, which allowed them to govern on a care and mainte-nance basis. The British established separate governments in Cyrenaica and in Tripolitania. Each province was divided into several districts governed by civil affairs officers, who reported to brigadiers at senior headquarters in Benghazi and Tripoli. They were non-political caretaker operations, at first trying to maintain peace and good order and to help the war effort. The Gaddafi regime was to cast this administration as imperialist and second only to the arch-enemy, the Italians.

It was long after the war when I met Major General Sir Duncan Cumming, KBE CBE OBE. He had been in charge of the British post-war administration of Cyrenaica. He played a pivotal role in the protracted and tortuous negotiations that led to the formation of the Kingdom of Libya. He certainly strove to bring internal self-government to Cyrenaica and his success in this regard set the standard for others. As personal influence is important in Libya, something of his background is worthy of attention.

I first met him in Tripoli in 1962. At that time he was the advisor on African affairs for British Overseas Airways. Later he came to Benghazi in that capacity, where I met him again in the way of duty. He drew my attention, for the first time, to the Bedouin tribes and their importance. He had an encyclopaedic knowledge of the people of Cyrenaica and could recite their lineage, a trait which endeared him to old-fashioned Libyans and which persuaded me that there was more to him than I had suspected. The last time I met him was in Port Moresby, Papua, when he was there to make a survey of aviation for the Australian administration of Papua New Guinea.

Duncan Cumming was educated at Giggleswick School and at Caius College, Cambridge. He was a Rugby Blue and played for England in the 1920s. From Cambridge he joined the Sudan Political Service.

He was later posted to Eritrea to command the British military government established there after the Italians had been removed in 1941. From thence he brought his experience of ex-Italian colonies to Benghazi as the chief administrator of the British military government of Cyrenaica in 1942. Here he did his best to train Libyans for their future role.

Major General Duncan Cumming in Cyrenaica, and his colleagues in the other provinces, were aware of the post-war plight of their Libyan charges. Thus they were forced by humanitarian and compassionate reasons to exceed their brief and attempt some small measures to improve law and order, medical care, local government, trade and education. Unlike Tripolitania, the infrastructure in Cyrenaica was shattered and efforts were made to restore port facilities, power supply, civilian travel, communications and postal services. One other point is that British subsidies, offered at a time when the cost of war was a serious burden at home, helped to sustain the impoverished Libyans in the period between the end of the war and independence, and for some time thereafter.

The Arab population was unaccustomed to the relative political freedom under the British military governments. Indeed, the British had some difficulty in persuading Cyrenaicans to adopt democratic principles. As a result of this they found it expedient to use the Senussi network throughout

tribal lands for local leadership. In this way the Senussi religious organisation was drafted into a political role.

In 1946 they made an attempt to promote self-government
with the formation of a national congress, with the Senussi
taking a leading role. What stirrings there were of wider
political interests were centred on 'the Omar Mukhtar Club',
named after the Senussi guerrilla leader.

In Tripolitania a more sophisticated populace more readily
engaged in politics, but found it hard to reach a consensus.
The Italian population of approximately 40,000 people was
a powerful factor to be considered and possible fascist sentiment created some anxiety. Some Arab families with business
interests which depended on the Italians complicated matters.

Most of these Italians had lived in Tripoli since the 1920s.
As independence approached, they still acted as though they
were running the country. The fascist salute was given and
returned. At the once famous automobile race track in Tripoli
fascist insignia still decorated what was the ex-governor's
private box. The rights of the Italians in Libya had still to be
clarified, a problem made the more difficult because the land
they worked and lived on was private property and there was
no immediate method of expropriation. It was clear that a too
rapid loss of the Italian population would be detrimental.

The emergent Tripolitanian political groups were deeply
concerned with the fear of dominance from Cyrenaica and
this preoccupation, one which is still alive today, tended to
take up much of their energies. They were, in the end, persuaded that acceptance of Senussi leadership was the best way
of forestalling a return of Italian rule.

In the Fezzan, the French did not encourage political activity. Though they were diligent in stimulating the economy,
their tendency to be dictatorial was resented. French troop
commanders acted in both military and civil capacities, as
they did in the Algerian Sahara. In the west of the Fezzan,
Ghat was attached to the French military region of southern
Algeria and Ghadames to the French command of southern
Tunisia. All this troubled Libyan nationalists, who feared that
the French might claim the Fezzan, which they had coveted
since the early nineteenth century when their North African
empire was expanding. The French retained control of the

Fezzan until Libya gained its independence and they maintained a small military presence there until at least 1958.

The Great Powers revisited the problem of Libya at the
Potsdam Conference in 1945. By this time the USA was
extending her strategic reach to counter the USSR. She now
recognised the importance of the Libyan ports and airfields to
her interests in the Mediterranean. This put a new emphasis
on Libya's future, with the USA now a major player.

In April 1945 the USA again entered the field with two
proposals. The first was that Libya should be returned to Italy.
The second was that Libya be partitioned into a Senussi emirate in Cyrenaica under British and Egyptian supervision, with
Tripolitania under an international trusteeship exercised by
the Italians. Neither of these plans gained support.

The continued effort to reach a solution to the Libya problem was handed over to the United Nations General Assembly
in September 1948. Therefore, the pressures of the Cold War
created differences that made for more delay. France and Britain
were notably reluctant to reach agreement. The Big Four
Council of foreign ministers sent a mission to Libya to gauge
the aspirations of the people, not before time it must be said.

Early in 1948, after three months of work on the ground,
the mission concluded that there was an overwhelming
desire for independence. Despite a Russian suggestion that
the French and British military governments should leave
immediately, the commission made it clear that Libya was too
impoverished economically, educationally, socially and politically for self-government.

Britain and Italy made another attempt to break the dead-
lock in 1949. Their respective foreign ministers, Ernest Bevin
and Count Sforza, proposed that Britain should assume the
trusteeship of Cyrenaica, Italy of Tripolitania and France
the Fezzan. The trusteeships were to last for ten years, when
Libya would seek UN approval for independence. The Bevin-
Sforza plan failed because the Libyans were not prepared to
accept Italian rule and demonstrated against it on the streets
of Tripoli and Benghazi with more than usual energy, secretly
egged on by the USSR and Egypt. For the first time, the
Libyan National Congress Party emerged. It made its views
clear and a consensus was reached in favour of independence.

The British now played a trump card. They unilaterally granted internal self-government to Cyrenaica, with Sayyid Idris as amir. When he had made a brief visit in 1944 he had been given rousing welcome. However, he had refused to return for good from exile in Egypt until the British had completely relinquished control. This gave Sayyid Idris a dominant role in the negotiations about Libya's future and neatly protected British interests.

The United Nations, somewhat constrained by the British move in Cyrenaica, now began to make plans for independence. It remained to be decided if the provinces would go their separate ways. Whatever the final outcome, the United Nations General Assembly, at its 250th plenary meeting on 21 November 1949, resolved that Libya would become:

> an independent and sovereign State … as soon as possible and not later than January 1, 1952, and that a constitution for Libya, including the form of the government, be determined by representatives of the inhabitants of Cyrenaica, Tripolitania, and the Fezzan, meeting and consulting together in a national assembly.[1]

This was to be the United Nations' first attempt to set up a sovereign state and there was some anxiety around at the time.

Another provision of the resolution was that there should be an interim administration, with a provisional native Cabinet supervised by a United Nations commissioner, Adrian Pelt of Holland, formerly an assistant secretary-general of the United Nations. He was to be guided by the advice of a United Nations Council for Libya. Sitting on this council were representatives of Egypt, France, Italy, Britain, Pakistan and the United States, and four native members representing Cyrenaica, Tripolitania, the Fezzan and Libyan minority groups. The United Nations resolutions were formulated in such a hurry that a number of critics doubted if many of the delegates who voted on this nation's future had any idea of the issues involved.

On 25 July 1950, Adrian Pelt invited twenty-one prominent Arabs – seven each from Cyrenaica and the Fezzan, six from Tripolitania and one representing the nation's minorities – to form a committee to discuss the composition of the National

Assembly and how to select its members. The committee decided that it should consist of twenty members from each of the three territories, to be appointed by the chiefs of the territories. Once established, the new National Assembly began drafting a constitution and making plans for a general election.

The discussions inevitably focused for some time on whether Libya should be a unified or a federal state. The possibility that one province would dominate a unitary government was a stumbling block not easily overcome. Gradually a compromise emerged, in which the Amir of Cyrenaica was to be invited to take the throne of a United Kingdom of Libya.

A Compromise

Thus it was that, in December 1950, the assembly passed a resolution proposing that the three provinces, the Fezzan, Tripolitania and Cyrenaica, should be combined under the crown of Sayyid Muhammad al Idris as-Senussi, Amir of Cyrenaica. However, the compromises buried within this resolution were to bedevil the country for some time.

I suspect that Sir Duncan Cumming was pleased with the outcome but hoped that Sayyid Idris would rally his subjects and give them a sense of national responsibility. Sayyid Idris had a wide religious following but a number of foes who criticised him for sitting out the Second World War in Egypt and for advocating that the French and British troops should remain in Libya. At the time, the French had a few Foreign Legion detachments in the Fezzan and the 1st British Infantry Division was in Tripolitania and Cyrenaica. The amir's relations with the neighbouring Egyptians were not particularly cordial, despite his long residence there.

A summary of the compromises that emerged from the various deliberations may be useful. Libya was to be a federal, constitutional, hereditary monarchy. There was to be a bicameral parliament. The House of Representatives was to be wholly elected, one deputy for every 20,000 male inhabitants, and the upper house, the Senate, was to be partially elected and partially appointed by the king. However, both parliament and the king could initiate legislation.

Parliament was to supply and appoint federal government ministers, who were to be responsible for foreign affairs and defence. The king was empowered to dismiss them. As a compromise, reached after fierce arguments, there were to be two capitals, Tripoli and Benghazi.

The three provinces were each to be governed by a wali (governor) appointed by the king and answerable to an elected legislative council based in their respective capitals, Tripoli, Benghazi and Sebha. In each province there was also to be an executive council, appointed by the king on the advice of the walis.

This arrangement led to a proliferation of bureaucracy and to endless disputes between provincial governments. The federal government was also hamstrung. It was forced to work from two capitals and with three provincial governments widely separated by geography and temperament, and bedevilled by intermittent telephone services. There were no telephone services at all within the towns of the Fezzan. The two capitals were more than 500 miles apart – a long way even in a powerful motorcar, as I was to find out for myself.

Disputes within and between the many centres of power were to be adjudicated by a supreme court. This required lawyers, of which there was an acute shortage. In the whole country there were but fifteen Libyans who had the benefit of a university education. The shortage of potential civil servants was acute.

The hope was that the nucleus of the British administrators then in Libya would stay on after independence on five-year contracts. Some, in fact, went home rather than take orders from Libyans of superior rank but no administrative experience. Others stayed because of a salary that went a long way in Libya – official cars, big houses, servants and cheap whisky. In contrast, Britain was a cold, demoralised and bleak country to live in at that time. Some, of course, found the work interesting. Instead of getting their salaries from the British Exchequer, the British advisors would get them from the Libyan Finance Minister, who would get part of his funds from the British Exchequer in any case. The United Nations was also to provide technical assistance and financial aid.

The task facing the new Libyan government in 1951 is almost beyond comprehension today. The Libyan people had been excluded from education, science, politics and even ordinary amenities, such as tap water, electricity, telephones and books. The skills necessary for commerce or government were absent. Adrian Pelt noted with regret the absence of women in work. This loss to the embryonic nation was enormous but, significantly, given less than its due attention.

It would be a long and painful process of education. Of the near 1 million Libyans alive at independence the majority were illiterate. The Western concept of co-operative effort, timekeeping and office hierarchy was alien. In Tripoli, a city with a population of 140,000, fewer than 7,000 of them read a daily newspaper. Of these, 4,500 read the Italian language *Corriere di Tripoli* and around 2,000 the Arab language *Tarabulus el Gharb*. Since the war, a good many Arabs had been killed or maimed because, in spite of repeated printed or oral warnings, they had collected live shells left lying around by Rommel's Africa Corps and Montgomery's 8th Army. Poverty drove them to build fires under the shells to make them explode. If they survived, they sold the casings in the scrap-metal market.

The rush to independence resulted in a number of compromises made for good reasons by good people. Hindsight allows us to discern which were mistakes. The most obvious error was the inadvertent concentration of power in the hands of the new king and his courtiers, a problem that was to come to light when oil was discovered.

Independence came with the growing presence of and dependence on the USA. Wheelus Field, near Tripoli, which had been used by the USAAF in 1943 as a bomber base and declared surplus in May 1947, was reactivated by the USAF Military Air Transport Service early in 1948. The Americans were beginning to recognise that the British military presence in Libya was likely to prove inadequate to counter the USSR and concluded that a large base in Libya was essential for their future strategic needs.

Wheelus Field had been leased by the United States government, part of it from the Libyan government and the rest from individual landholders, for a sum that was to increase after independence.

Independent Libya would need all the money it could get. Tax revenue was insufficient to meet its expenses. What is more, there were different currencies in each of the provinces: Egyptian pounds in Cyrenaica; Algerian francs in the Fezzan; and the British army military authority lire (MAL) in Tripolitania. A common Libyan currency was established. Another service the British did for the emergent Libya was to back a substantial percentage of the new currency by bringing Libya within the sterling area.

Britain and, to a lesser extent, France had quietly subsidised in Libya during the process of state building. The choice was clear, but eventually unpopular. In the absence of any other possible income, it would be necessary for Libya to reach long-term agreements with Britain and the USA, though not France, in which aid and rental income was provided in return for the presence of foreign military bases on Libyan soil.

A factor, which was not without influence, was the growing Arab nationalism. The USA and Britain were anxious to ensure that their rights to bases in Libya were secured before she came under pressure from other Arab states to evict them. The Israeli question was to continue to affect the relationship between Libya, the USA and Britain.

On 24 December 1951 Sayyid Muhammad al Idris as-Senussi stood on the balcony of the al Mahar palace, Benghazi, next to his new prime minister, Mahmoud Muntasir, as he proclaimed the creation of the United Kingdom of Libya, the first and last state created by the General Assembly of the United Nations. Muntasir was an Italian-educated businessman who was pro-Italian and, during the Second World War, pro-German.

7

The Kingdom of Libya
The Shepherd King and the Oil Barons

King Idris was never happy away from his remote home amongst the tribes of Cyrenaica, to which he retired too often. He was old and rather frail when he gained power and some of his entourage were unscrupulous. His was not a belligerent reign, but it was caught out in the end in the revolutionary zeal of the time.

His adherence to Britain and latterly to the USA was severely criticised by his successors, but he had little choice in the matter. He needed Western technology and expertise to prospect for oil and bring it to the markets of the world.

He was unfairly accused of corruption by his successors, but the truth is that he was unable to control his courtiers who were the real culprits. His inability to produce a male heir was unhelpful.

Two of our friends in Benghazi visited King Idris and Queen Fatima al Senussi in Tobruk in the course of their duties. I am grateful to them for their sympathetic view of the royal couple, which I have tried to convey here. They both noted that the queen was tolerant and charming. She did what she could to promote the cause of women in Libya and frequently wore Western clothes in public. She was devoted to her husband and the vicissitudes of her life reflect the strange history of his reign. He was a devout Muslim, frugal man and a skilled negotiator who knew the value of patience.

The king had been vested with great personal power when Libya achieved independence. He exercised much of that power through the members of the royal household, the diwan. He was too trusting of his closest advisors. To be fair, and as events were to prove, he did not personally make huge profits from corruption, for which he was later to be condemned.

He was not happy in Tripoli. The royal palace had been the residence of the Italian governor and was ostentatious. I entered it once and confirm that it would not have suited the king's frugal taste, for which he was often ridiculed by the sophisticated Tripolitanians. His preference for living in the Gebel Akhdar had practical consequences, which made life difficult. Since the king maintained a residence in Baida, the town was to become the de facto federal capital of Libya for a while. Its remoteness was a handicap. It was always difficult to contact government officials by phone and, whilst the little railway from Benghazi terminated there, the journey was more picturesque than convenient.

Some say that the small palace in Tobruk, even further from Tripoli, was favoured as a residence by the king and queen because it was near the Royal Air Force station at el Adem, a British base, from which they might be evacuated if they were threatened. An equally persuasive argument was that Queen Fatima and King Idris were not keen on regal trappings and liked to live frugally surrounded by the tribes that they trusted. The proximity of the Egyptian border and the strength of the Senussi sect amongst the tribes in the Egyptian Western Desert may have offered a reassuringly quick way of retiring from the trials of kingship. Tobruk, though famous as a site of heroic battles during the Second World War, was certainly a very frugal sort of town when I visited during the 1960s. A final and damning argument was that the king was avoiding his duties.

As the sympathetic obituarist of *The Times* wrote after her death on 3 October 2009, the life of Sayyida Fatima al Shi'fa binti Sayyid Ahmad as Sherif al Senussi 'was intimately bound up with the creation of modern Libya, and accordingly framed by exile'. She was born in Kufra in 1911 and was the daughter of Ahmad al Sherif, the third leader of the Senussi sect. Fatima never knew the exact date of her birth.

The remoteness of Kufra, one of a number of oases deep in Libya, was amongst its attractions for her father. It is largely protected by the Ribiana Sand Sea to its north-west and the Kalansho Sand Sea to its north-east. The track from Benghazi, the old slave trade route, passes the oases of Tazerbo and Zighen and then the gap in the sand seas to Kufra proper.

In 1941, the famous desert explorer and soldier Colonel R.A. Bagnold described the oasis complex thus:

> Imagine northern Europe as a rainless desert of sand and rock, with London as Tag (the site of the fort in Kufra proper), a little area a few miles across, with shallow artesian well water, palm groves, villages and salt lakes, and with a population of 4,000. The suburb of Tazerbo with another 1,000 inhabitants is north-west where Liverpool is. Zighen would be near Derby, and Rebiana near Bristol cut off by a sea of dunes. Cairo would be at Copenhagen, across a sand sea. Wadi Halfar (on the Nile) would be near Munich, with waterless desert in between.[1]

In 1929 Fatima was forced to flee Kufra on camelback to escape the attack by the notorious Italian Rudolfo Graziani, whose military units had penetrated as far as Kufra with the intention of massacring its Senussi community. She never forgot the seventeen-day trek across the desert to safety in Egypt.

In 1931 she was married to the grandson of the first Grand Senussi, Sayyid Muhammad al Idris as-Senussi, at the famous oasis of Siwa in Egypt. He was some twenty years her senior and had been married three times. All the children of his first marriages had died in infancy and it was his great hope to produce an heir. Fatima was to suffer many miscarriages and brought but one son to full term. He lived for only one day. Her failure to produce a direct heir was to cause her much trouble.

She remained in Egypt with Sayyid Idris until he returned to Cyrenaica. He had made provision for his exile out of the payments made to him by the Italian government. Nevertheless, it must have been a trying and impoverished exile. His position was a difficult one and in his absence the Senussi organisation in Libya was all but destroyed.

As queen, Fatima lived for much of the time in the summer palace in Tobruk. It was a modest bungalow, having but a few rooms that were heated in the winter by a charcoal brazier. The marriage was soon to be severely tested. As she failed to produce an heir, tensions grew. The king's close favourite and long-term advisor was Ibrahim al Shelhi, whose ambitions were limitless. The royal entourage became unsettled by the credible rumour that the king was to divorce Fatima and marry al Shelhi's daughter.

In October 1954 the queen's nephew, al Sherif, driven to excess by the rumours, murdered Ibrahim al Shelhi in a street in Benghazi. The king was appalled and had him executed, and a number of royal princes exiled to the Fezzan. He was so upset by these events that he retreated to Tobruk, avoiding the royal residences in Tripoli and Benghazi as much as possible. Ibrahim's eldest son, Busairi, became the king's most trusted advisor.

King Idris, seriously concerned about the succession, was soon persuaded to exercise his right to have more than one wife and marry a woman whose fecundity might solve his dynastic problems. Fatima suggested two possible candidates but the king rejected them in favour of a mature Egyptian lady whom he married in 1955. The union was not successful and Fatima, who was never divorced, clung to the royal bungalow in Tobruk and was soon reinstated as queen and companion.

The king's attempts to solve the succession problem by fathering a male heir were unsuccessful and the heir apparent, his brother, Mohamad al Rida, died in 1955. Mohamad's second son, Hassan al Rida, was appointed Crown prince. The Crown Prince Hassan lacked personality and even favourable observers suggested that he was not well suited to be king.

During their marriage, Queen Fatima and King Idris were kind enough to bring up a number of young relatives and also adopted an Algerian girl whose father had been killed fighting the French. Significantly, they also remained loyal to the al Shelhi family. One of them, Omar al Shelhi, was later to be involved with the oil business and some of his dealings reflected badly on the king.

In 1968 he married the daughter of the Libyan prime minister of the time. King Idris was the best man and made Omar Minister of Palace Affairs. It was Omar's brother, Abdul Aziz al Shelhi, who became chief of staff of the Libyan army. These two men were to exercise extraordinary power and patronage.

King Idris derived much of his support from the tribes amongst which he chose to live. He carefully structured his

1. Hassan Karamanli, Bey of Tripoli. He was murdered by his brother Yusuf, who became Bashaw of Tripoli and provoked the USA into a war in 1801. (From *A Ten Year's Residence at the Court of Tripoli*, Miss Tully, sister-in-law of British consul Richard Tully, Henry Colburn, 1819)

2. Tripoli castle as it was at the time of the Karamanli dynasty, 1711 to 1835. (Seaton Dearden)

3. Ottoman janissary aghas (army officers) at leisure, showing their various uniforms. (From *A Ten Year's Residence at the Court of Tripoli*, Miss Tully, sister-in-law of British consul Richard Tully, Henry Colburn, 1819)

4. Chromolithograph of the Italo-Turkish war peace treaty, 1912. (Lombardi Historical Collection/ Wikimedia Commons)

5. The Libyan guerrilla leader Omar Mukhtar in chains after his capture in 1931. Gaddafi wore a copy of this photograph as a badge when he attended conferences. (Wikimedia Commons)

6. Omar Mukhtar's tomb, Benghazi, Libya. (Wikimedia Commons)

Top to bottom:
7. An aerial view of the royal palace in Tripoli in 1957. King Idris (and the author) found it too ostentatious. It was built during the Italian occupation of Libya. (Peter Cox collection)

8. Tripoli castle in 1957. The facade had been restored by the Italians. At the time when this photograph was taken the apartments of the Ottoman rulers of Tripoli could still be seen inside the castle. (Peter Cox)

9. A suburb of Tripoli where the author lived in 1958. (Peter Cox)

10. The Second World War. British army Bren gun carriers advancing across open desert in 1940. (Author's collection)

11. Part of a rare picture of French native cavalry crossing the desert in the Fezzan (now South Libya) with the Free French in 1940. This was the forgotten campaign led by General Leclerc, which cleared the Axis forces from Southern Libya. (Christian de la Chappelle)

12. Sayyid Ahmed al Sherif, Senussi leader, who fought the French, the Italians and, during the Great War, the British. (Macaluso)

13. Sayyid Muhammad Idris bin Muhammad al Mahdi as-Senussi, King of Libya from 1951 to 1969. (Evans-Pritchard)

14. A village outside Benghazi showing the real poverty that so many Libyans experienced before oil was found. The village was called Tin Town by the British because the houses were constructed out of corrugated iron. (Peter Cox)

15. A sheikh of one of the nine Sa'adi tribes of Eastern Libya displaying his horsemanship in 1957. (Peter Cox)

16. The Colonial War Graves Commission Cemetery at Tobruk, East Libya. British and Commonwealth soldiers killed during the Second World War Siege of Tobruk are buried here. (Maureen Norgate)

17. A view of the ancient Greek and Roman ruins of Cyrene in the Green Mountains (the Gebel Akhdar) of East Libya. The city gave its name to the old Libyan province of Cyrenaica. (Maureen Norgate)

18. The Berenice Hotel in Benghazi, Eastern Libya, in the 1960s. The domed cathedral close by was built during the Italian colonial period. Berenice was the name of the ancient Greek city on the ruins of which modern Benghazi is built. (Maureen Norgate)

19. A very rare view of the palace of King Idris in Tobruk, taken from the harbour. It was the king's favourite residence and he retreated to it during times of crisis. (Maureen Norgate)

armed forces to counter a possible military coup. We have seen how the Libyan Arab Force was raised in Egypt during the Second World War. When the war in Libya was over there was no longer any need for it. Many of its officers and men were reluctant to disband and found employment in the police force under the British military government. They had formed the nucleus of the Royal Libyan Army after independence.

The king, however, was wary of a powerful army. As a counterbalance he raised an elite armed police force, the Cyrenaican Defence Force. This force was officered by trusted allies of the king and recruited from tribes that were notably loyal to him. The Cyrenaican Defence Force was originally trained by British military specialists and stationed at strategic places around Cyrenaica. A Tripolitanian Defence Force was also formed along similar lines. Whilst the army was to grow during the period of the kingdom, it was never allowed to be larger than the armed police forces.

The first test of the constitution came in February 1952 during the first general election. Tripolitania was more populous than Cyrenaica and the Fezzan and, therefore, had thirty-five constituencies out of a total of fifty-five. The National Congress Party fielded a candidate in all of the Tripolitanian constituencies. Had it won all or a sufficient majority of the seats, it would have been able to amend the constitution. In the event, it gained only a few seats. The spectre of vote rigging was raised and caused violent riots in Tripoli. They were suppressed by the police who shot to kill.

The National Congress Party in Tripolitania, the Omar Mukhtar Club in Cyrenaica and all other political groups were outlawed. Only candidates acceptable to the government, effectively the king's advisors, were permitted to stand for election from this date. It was said the unacceptable candidates were arrested on the day they were required to register as such. This was not a constitutional monarchy and a parliamentary democracy.

Britain and the USA had squatters' rights to their military bases. The next test of Libya's government was to focus around them. King Idris had long ago thrown in his lot with the British. He was now confronted with the dilemmas inherent in Arab nationalism and the burgeoning anti-British movement in post-war Egypt. There was an added dimension, which is not often taken into account by historians.

Britain's imperial role was diminishing and she was becoming a lesser player alongside the USA in the Cold War. In Britain there was a growing change in the attitude to British bases in Egypt and the Mediterranean. The post-war Labour Foreign Secretary, Ernest Bevin, had reached an agreement with the Egyptian government which accepted, in principle, the total evacuation of British troops from Egypt. His prime minister, Clement Attlee, was later to remark: 'But India had ceased to be an Imperial place of arms and the Suez Canal had never been a good waterway; and the idea of the Mediterranean as a covered passage for Britain had also been exploded.'[2]

The Conservative government of Winston Churchill, which followed Atlee into power in 1951, rejected this view and commenced on the path that would lead to the Suez crisis in 1956. It should be remembered, however, that the British Labour government was in power during the protracted period of state building in Libya and its attitude was surely clear to King Idris and his diwan. This must have led to a lack of confidence in Britain's long-term commitment to Libya and would have been taken into consideration by the new Libyan government after independence.

Behind all this, the drum beat of the Palestine problem was audible and the Arab world was mobilising against the new state of Israel, with the formation of the Arab League. The revolution in Egypt in 1952 was, eventually, to bring Nasser to power. Libya could not avoid embroilment in the problem for long.

King Idris solved the dilemma by joining the Arab League and also by signing a twenty-year treaty with Britain in 1953. The British military bases in Libya were thus secure until 1973. In 1954 an agreement with the USA, giving the Americans the use of Wheelus Air Force Base until 1970, was also signed, but not without opposition both inside and outside Libya.

In the 1953 treaty in return for bases, the British offered Libya subsidies, weapons and help if Egypt invaded. This last was an inflammatory clause and it was as well that some parts of the treaty agreement were secret. The USA became the biggest donor of aid and it is estimated that she spent more than $100 million by the end of 1959.[3] The income arising from the UK and USA agreements were to provide the first windfall for Libya. To emphasise a point, Libya's income was not raised from taxes. It arose from Libya's strategic value to the USA and the UK. Thus the Libyans, with the exception of a few workers on the bases, were not engaged in earning it. The source of the income, or the need for it, was not apparent to many Libyans.

A disconcerting sidelight is cast upon Libya by Edward J. Epstein. He states that the construction by the United States of the Wheelus Field Air Force Base was a '$110 million project that was designed for ten thousand troops and technicians'. He goes on to assert that 'a major source of income for the new Libya bureaucracy was systematically collecting kickbacks from the project's subcontractors, making the government in the eyes of one US diplomat, the most corrupt in the world'.[4] The problem of corruption was to bedevil Libya for some time.

There was one other event that had a lasting effect on Libya, but which received little attention at the time. Nasser sent one of his close associates, Major General Ahmed Hassan el Faki, as the Egyptian ambassador to Libya. El Faki arranged for over 500 Egyptian teachers to work in Libya, drawing salaries from Egypt as well as Libya. He also arranged for army personnel from Egypt to be seconded to Libya, including a senior officer. The teachers were to have a notable effect on young Libyan minds, not least on the young Muammar Gaddafi.[5]

Oil is Found Below the Desert

Libya's long-term prospects suddenly changed. Before the Second World War had interrupted them, the Italians were quietly looking for oil in the Sirtica, where it sometimes contaminated water wells. In 1955 a survey commissioned by the United Nations located oil-bearing formations below the Libyan Desert. A number of oil companies were granted permission to explore further. Esso found oil in the Sirte basin and other companies followed suit. The oil was low in sulphur and light, but it was waxy, a limitation which became apparent at low temperatures.

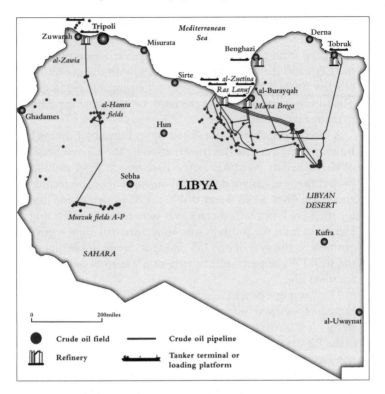

The crude oil pipelines, oil ports and refineries in Libya as they were before the 2011 uprising. It is noted that the great majority of these are within East Libya, which fell to the anti-Gaddafi forces in early 2011.

There were advantages. Pipelines from the Libyan oil fields to the sea would not have to cross other countries. Thus there would be no malicious attempts by another power to shut them down. What is more, Libyan oil did not have to be shipped via the Suez Canal or round the Cape of Good Hope.

On the advice of the UN, a number of foreign experts were employed to draft what became the Libyan Petroleum Act of 1955. They set out to break the hold of the large oil companies, which acted as a cartel. The act they forged was unique and clever, leaving only one loophole.

At the time, the oil business was largely tied up by a consortium known as the Seven Sisters. It was launched in 1928 by Royal Dutch Shell, Standard Oil of New Jersey (Esso, later Exxon) and Anglo-Persian Oil (BP). Instead of bidding against each other for oil concessions, they agreed to co-operate and apportion the oil that they found amongst themselves in accordance with an agreed formula. Later the consortium was expanded to include Standard Oil of California (Chevron), Standard Oil of New York (Mobil), Texas Company (Texaco) and Gulf Oil. The Seven Sisters agreed to share their pipelines, refineries, tankers and marketing facilities. A country with potential oilfields was at the cartel's mercy. Wherever oil was discovered, the Seven Sisters, who alone had the wherewithal to do so, set up a local company which offered to exploit it. If a government tried to argue, they withdrew the services of their tankers and their refineries. The key point is that the Sevens Sisters controlled the posted price of oil without consulting the oil-producing countries.

Libya needed the Seven Sisters, so it devised a way of attracting and also controlling them. The Libyan Petroleum Act of 1955 divided the oil-bearing regions into eighty-four separate concessions of 30,000 square kilometres in the north and 80,000 square kilometres in the south. It allowed the companies to bid separately for each concession, but restricted the number allowed to one company. The successful companies were to release one-quarter of their concessions in the fifth year of operation and a further quarter in the eighth year. More releases were required in the tenth year. The taxes on oil produced were set so that the Libyan government might benefit by up to 50 per cent of net production after the companies' exports reached an agreed level.

There was one interesting rider added to the Petroleum Act. It was that Petroleum Commission, responsible for awarding oil concessions, was to take account of how the bidder proposed to work in the public interest. The strategy depended on making it possible for independent oil companies, such as Hunt Oil and Phillips, to acquire concessions. The first concessions, however, were awarded to Esso, British Petroleum, Texaco and Chevron.

In the meantime, affairs in neighbouring Egypt began to affect Libya. On 26 July 1956, Nasser announced the nationalisation of the Suez Canal. On 29 October 1956, General

Moshe Dyan led the Israeli army in an attack on Egypt. The British and the French invasion forces followed two days later, landing in Port Said. On 5 November they took the city and advanced towards the Suez Canal. Nasser blocked the canal and the Arab world was up in arms. The USA and USSR made their opposition to the attack clear and the invading forces were called off. It was an ignominious defeat for the British and especially for the British prime minister, Anthony Eden, who resigned office soon after the event.

For the United Kingdom of Libya this was not a good time. King Idris had aligned his government too firmly with the British. There were large British army and Royal Air Force units stationed in Libya. They could have been used in the invasion of Egypt. In fact, some were being sent there secretly via Cyprus.[6]

There were serious anti-British riots in Tripoli and Benghazi. That Britain was no longer an invincible imperial power was not lost on the young Muammar Gaddafi. King Idris survived the crisis but it was a grave test of his pro-British policy. The British lost a great deal more than the short war. Their greatest asset had been respect, something which is hard to quantify. So much was lost in this one incident that it marked a real turning point in Britain's relationship with the Arab world. It also diminished the power of King Idris in Libya.

On 12 April 1959 Esso made a major strike in the Zelten field, a hundred miles or so south of the coast of the Gulf of Sirte. The company built a pipeline through the desert and a big oil port at Marsa Brega. In the autumn of 1961 the company started pumping good oil into the *Esso Canterbury*, the first of their large oil tankers to load in Libya. Others were queuing up behind her in the Gulf of Sirte. There was a huge quantity of oil under the desert. The oil terminal at Es Sidra was opened in 1962 and at Ras Lanuf in 1964.

In 1961 I was interviewed by Abdul Majid Kubar, sometime prime minister of Libya. I was posted from Tripoli to Benghazi where something had gone very wrong and he wanted to be sure I knew what I was getting myself into. He impressed me greatly.

When in government he had decreed that 70 per cent of the oil revenue would be used for development projects which would benefit the people. In 1960 a development council had been set up and plans were made to build houses, improve agriculture and expand the infrastructure. Sadly, the patronage inherent in the great wealth led to corruption on a grand scale.

When he interviewed me, he had not long been out of office. His government had given a large contract to Sayyid Abdullah Abid, a friend of one of Kubar's predecessors and of the al Shelhi family of courtiers. The contract was for building a road from Tripoli deep into the Fezzan. It was given to Abid despite costing a great deal more than the original estimate. There were accusations of corruption which tainted even Abdul Majid Kubar's staff. In my view an honest man, Kubar went to the king and resigned.

King Idris had been under pressure for a long time to ditch the federal system in favour of a unitary government. The advent of oil made it impetrative but difficult to achieve in practice. Most of the oil was found in Cyrenaica and this evened up the balance of power between the provinces. The king was finally persuaded that the government, under pressure to spend the oil revenues effectively, would work better if Libya abandoned the federal system. Consequently, a constitutional amendment of 1963 abolished the federal formula and brought in a unified state apparatus. The power of the national government was enhanced and the provincial legislative assemblies, bureaucracies and judicial systems were disbanded.

King Idris now had the right to make appointments to local administrative councils and choose the country's senators. The oil revenues now accrued solely to central government. A central bank was included in these reforms and its governor reported directly to the royal diwan. The end result was a further concentration of power in the hands of the king or, more accurately, the royal diwan. The United Kingdom of Libya became the Kingdom of Libya and the chief of police was appointed from the Cyrenaican Defence Force, the paramilitary unit most loyal to the king.[7]

In 1963, the government of King Idris formed the Libyan National Oil Company. The context in which this important step was taken was this: the oil-producing countries, especially in the Arab world, had decided to reduce the power of the Seven Sisters and had formed the Organisation of Petroleum

Exporting Countries (OPEC) in 1959. OPEC made it clear that it expected the oil companies to consult with it when setting oil prices.

The question it next addressed was whether the oil-producing countries could find, produce and market oil themselves. A longer term plan was needed. In addition to Libya, Iran, Kuwait and Saudi Arabia all established their own national oil companies in the 1960s.

The Libyan Petroleum Law allowed for the joint operation of concessions. The entry fee, the official amount paid upfront for a concession, was relatively low compared to that charged by other countries. This attracted some of the great characters of the oil industry. The Texan whom I found early one morning in 1963 sitting on the wall between our villas in Benghazi, shooting sparrows with an air rifle, was to have an enormous influence on the price you and I pay for petrol today. George Williamson kept chickens in his backyard and argued that each sparrow he killed saved him 35 Libyan piastres, as that was the value in hen food it would otherwise consume. At the time he was shooting sparrows on our joint wall George, known as Bud, worked for Nelson Bunker Hunt.

Nelson Bunker Hunt had bid for, and won, an oil concession in Libya. He formed a partnership with British Petroleum, called BP Bunker Hunt, which was to operate the field. George Williamson was Nelson's man in Libya to keep an eye on BP. Later he was to work for another larger-than-life character, Armand Hammer, but first the Bunker Hunt story.

BP Bunker Hunt prospered. In February 1967 a ceremony was held when King Idris opened an oil port at Marsa Hariga, 2 miles from Tobruk. As a gift, Nelson Bunker Hunt presented the king with a gold key. BP Bunker Hunt had built a crude-oil pipeline 320 miles long from oil wells in the Sarir concession to Marsa Hariga. It was buried 6ft below the ground in order to keep the oil liquid when the temperature dropped during the nights. By now the oil was flowing from wells in the desert to a number of terminals on Libya's Mediterranean shore and she was seventh, behind the USA, USSR, Venezuela, Saudi Arabia, Kuwait and Iran, in world oil production, and thirty-nine companies were operating in the Libyan Desert pumping more than 1.7 million barrels a day.

King Idris was 76 when he opened the BP Bunker Hunt facility near Tobruk and was becoming more than ever a reluctant king. His problems had been mounting steadily. In hindsight, it is easy to see where they began. The story of Armand Hammer's dealings in Libya suggests that corruption was one of the major fault lines.

The accusations made against Armand Hammer by Edward J. Epstein in his book *Dossier, The Secret History of Armand Hammer* are based on wide research, but he makes some mistakes in detail which must be taken into account. Since my sometime neighbour, George Williamson, left Bunker Hunt and went to work for Hammer I will confine what follows to those parts of Epstein's findings that survive the closest scrutiny.

Armand Hammer formed a company called Occidental Petroleum, with which he proposed to enter the oil business in Libya, and used the clause in the Petroleum Law that allowed public interest matters, called Elements of Preference, to influence the adjudicators in his favour. The clause led to companies offering sweeteners to help make their bids attractive. According to Dirk Vandewalle: 'In one of the best known sweeteners, Occidental ... outbid 20 other companies in 1966. As part of its contract it agreed to spend 5% of its pre-tax profits ... to drill for water around the Kufra oasis – an area of historical importance to the Senusi [sic] monarchy.'[8]

Edward J. Epstein goes to great length to prove that Hammer also contracted to pay a substantial sum to a high-placed 'fixer' to ensure that the Occidental bid was successful and that the water-drilling clause was inserted to give him leverage.[9] I can confirm that there were rumours of unusual contractual arrangements being made during this period and that there was also talk of a 3 per cent overriding royalty being demanded by some influential persons. Occidental struck oil in abundance and by 1968, in company with Bechtel, had built a crude oil pipeline from its field and opened an oil terminal at Zuetina.

In July 1960, King Idris had written a pubic letter condemning corruption, in which he referred to 'reports of the misconduct of responsible state personnel taking bribes – in secret and in public ...'. The letter seems to have been ignored by members of his entourage, which, to quote Vandewalle again, included too many individuals for whom personal enrichment had become an all-consuming passion. The king was controlled by his diwan and was unable to agree to the reforms that might have saved him.

Discontent and Plots

The build-up of discontent was manifested in a number of riots. I witnessed a few of them in Benghazi during 1964 and 1965. In February 1964, Nasser's propaganda machine was focusing on Libya. Egyptian radio began to state that British troops from Libya had been used illegally in the Suez invasion in 1956. Cairo was demanding the immediate removal of British soldiers from Libyan soil on the grounds that they posed a threat to Egypt and, thus, supported Israel. The Egyptian Embassy encouraged students to demonstrate against the British and so they took to the streets. The Egyptians paid shoeshine boys to throw a few stones to warm things up and matters got out of hand. Shots were fired and the caretaker of my office was killed by a stray police bullet.

In June 1967, the Israelis struck rapidly against a build-up of Egyptian troops in what is now known as the Six Day War. Severe and prolonged anti-British and anti-US riots broke out in Tripoli and Benghazi and got seriously out of control. Government workers struck and closed the oil terminals. The government announced that it would demand the evacuation of British and American bases from Libya. A number of young Libyan army officers were boiling with frustration.

According to Blundy and Lycett, a contingent of Libyan soldiers was sent to help the Egyptians but was too late. Gaddafi was said to have been amongst them.[10] This was interpreted by an angry public as a last-ditch attempt to save King Idris, but it was too late. The Islamic world was shocked and distressed when, in August 1969, an Australian blew up the al Asqa mosque in Jerusalem. During the period between 1967 and August 1969, Libyans were aroused to an unprecedented level of anger.

There is a great deal of controversy surrounding the king's role in the dying days of the Kingdom of Libya. By 1979 he was old and tired. To my knowledge, he had attempted to abdicate at least once before and was dissuaded by his diwan with the aid of a tribal demonstration of support. In 1969, his dilemma was serious. It is likely that he was clear-sighted enough to see that Crown Prince Hassan was not capable of replacing him and had realised that his favourite, Omar al Shelhi, was tainted by corruption. I am sure that he was aware that a number of factions were plotting a coup and may had decided to pre-empt them.

There were a number of interested parties, most of whom were sure there would be a coup. The Americans were watchful because their oil companies were heavily committed and their base at Wheelus was still important for their strategic plans. The CIA was represented in Libya at the time and it is strange that it could have no knowledge of the various plotters.

The Americans may have assumed that the British diplomats were *au courant* with the possible plotters and might be relied on to arrange for the Royal Enniskillen Fusiliers, who were stationed just outside Benghazi at the time, to intervene if the wrong coup took place. Both the British and the Americans were anxious to keep Nasser's hands off the oilfields.

I suspect that Nasser's men in Libya were confident that the outcome would be in their favour. One aspect which may have some relevance is that Nasser was by now ill and tired. His revolution had almost run its course in Egypt and his personal grip on events was loosening.

Amongst the most plausible of the speculations that surround the last days of the reign of King Idris is that he, like many others, knew there was an army coup in the offing. The hypothesis is that he expected Aziz al Shelhi, the army chief of staff, to mount it and so decided to leave Libya to allow him a free hand. Aziz al Shelhi was, however, the brother of Omar al Shelhi, who was by now thought to be thoroughly corrupt.

The king decided to take himself off to a spa in Turkey for medical treatment and a rest. He was determined to abdicate and hoped to retire to the summer palace in Tobruk. He called his prime minister and the head of the senate to Turkey and handed them the instrument of abdication, naming the Crown prince as his successor. It was to take effect on 1 September 1969.

The arrangement was forestalled by the young army officers surrounding Muammar Gaddafi, who were to assume power on behalf of the people. There was no real way of asking the people.

The king was left high and dry in Turkey, with no money to pay his hotel bills, which the Turkish government kindly settled. He went to Egypt and died in 1983. He is buried in Medina, Saudi Arabia. His government in Libya had achieved success in a number of fields, notably in education, for which it has received little recognition. The country he took over lacked expertise and infrastructure. He was at first forced to rely on the British and American military bases and aid as a source of income. He also needed Western technology and expertise to find and exploit the oil beneath the desert, and his government had handled the oil companies wisely and well.

However, he was tired, old and weak.[11] He had not wanted to be king of all Libya and the great powers that had been thrust upon him were exercised by a small group of people who let him down in the end. The formation of the state of Israel, and then an unwise decision by the British to go to war against Egypt over the Suez Canal, raised a revolutionary fervour amongst some young Libyans.

8

Gaddafi I
Companions
of the Tent

The exercise of great power for long periods by a single individual warps the political fabric of a nation and the machinery of government becomes the monopoly of a small group of people that project the personality of its leader. Gaddafi was but 27 years old when he came to power. His formative years are, therefore, more than usually important.

He was born a Bedouin, whose family was psychologically and physiologically adapted to the extreme conditions of desert living. The life of a true Bedouin is so far removed from the way we live in the West that it is almost beyond comprehension. Here, I have attempted to lift a small corner of the tent on Gaddafi's nurture and early life.

The young men who left their Bedouin tents or isolated oases to live in Libya's cities in the middle of the twentieth century journeyed there from a culture largely unchanged for centuries. Muammar Abu Minyar al Gaddafi and many of those who joined him in the military coup in 1969 were to share in this experience. They must have called upon vast resources of intelligence and adaptability to achieve what they did. However, they were the prisoners of the culture that nurtured them, as are we all. Some of the serious misjudgements they made are partially explained by the profound cultural isolation in which they were brought up, compared to the modern world in which they exercised power.

Historians are permitted to look for explanations for the behaviour of historical personages amongst events which occurred during their childhood and adolescence. Perhaps it will thus be possible to discern the origins of Gaddafi's dangerous tendency to oversimplify and his controversial actions whilst in power.

The old Italian colonial road had been built around the shores of the Gulf of Sirte, which thrusts its way into the desert. If you look at the map, you can see that there are really two Gulfs of Sirte, the lesser and the greater. The map makes them look like two successive mouthfuls taken out of the north coast of Libya. The road is long and the desert desolate and, if you allow yourself to think too much, it is very intimidating. At the southern reach of the gulf is the town of Sirte.

When I was in the region in 1961, Sirte's isolation was truly stunning. Gaddafi was born here, in one of the tents of the Gaddadfa tribe, which made its meagre living in the harsh desert hinterland. Recollections of his birthplace, the Bedouin ways of his parents and the importance of the tribe in his culture have been built up in his memory and self-edited over the years to establish his personal narrative, the personal story he carries in his head.

Here is the narrative, as it emerged in 2002, which Gaddafi had prepared for public consumption. On 2 November of that year, he was interviewed in his tent in Bab Azzizia by Professor Edmond Jouve. The transcript of the interview appears in *My Vision* by Muammar Gaddafi and Edmond Jouve. Gaddafi is reported to have said: 'I was born in a tent in the desert in September 1942. There was no doctor or midwife present. I went to school fairly late. I didn't give it any thought. I was guarding the herds, sowing the seed, cultivating the land.' This is a summary of the life of an adolescent boy in a Bedouin tent, though some of the tasks described would have been reserved for older boys. In the same interview Gaddafi implies that he and his family were not aware of the concept of a state or a government. Perhaps so – the tribes were subject to benign neglect by government at the time.

In his *Green Book*, written as a manifesto, Gaddafi devotes two sections to the tribe. He argues that the tribe 'is a social school where its members are brought up from childhood to absorb high ideals which will be transformed into a behaviour pattern for life ... the tribe provides for its members ... collective payment of ransom, collective fines, collective revenge and collective defence'.[1]

In his interview with Professor Jouve, Gaddafi recalls the Second World War and he describes exploding mines, flying bullets and aerial bombardments. These would have been folk memories, for he would have been too young to be an eyewitness, unless he had falsified his birth date. That he did not understand the reason for it all is not surprising. It was a war fought in Libya between foreigners for reasons that the tribesmen would not have welcomed. 'Those were my earliest childhood memories,' Gaddafi told Professor Jouve. That they were not accurate is of little consequence. They formed part of his core person and affected his adult behaviour.[2]

Ronald Bruce St John writes that when he lived in his parent's tent Gaddafi was given some religious education by a tribal teacher.[3] If that is so, and St John is consistently accurate, this will have taken the form of rote learning. Probably at the age of 10, Gaddafi left the family tent and enrolled in the primary school in Sirte. He made good progress but was ridiculed because he was a Bedouin. He later moved to Sebha in the Fezzan, where his father took a post as a caretaker guarding a prominent citizen's property. Gaddafi entered a secondary school in the town and embarked on a revolutionary career. He came into contact with Egyptian teachers and under the influence of Nasser's 'Voice of the Arabs' on the radio.

He was expelled from the school in Sebha and there are conflicting stories as to why. They all focus on his political activity, which consisted of giving speeches, distributing leaflets and, some say, being gratuitously rude to an English school inspector. Whatever the reason, he moved to a secondary school in Misurata, where he met a number of his fellow conspirators with whom he was to overthrow the king. He is said to have formed the nucleus of his revolutionary band of officers here. They all decided to obtain commissions in the army, which they proposed to take over, use as the instrument of their coup and as their power base afterwards.

'The Arab has received the message and force of modern history at one blow; it has come from outside and it has not been spread over three or four centuries.'[4] The cultural gulf, which the young Gaddafi and his fellow revolutionaries crossed between the Bedouin tents and the two major Libyan cities, Tripoli and Benghazi, was wide indeed. We might profitably step back over that gulf to understand Gaddafi a little better.

When he came to power Gaddafi was sometimes ridiculed because he pitched his Bedouin tent near his home in Bab Azzizia and frequently threatened to cart it around with him on international trips. It caused consternation wherever he proposed to take it. It was hard to find a place safe enough for it in Cairo or New York without risking some sort of security or sanitary incident. In reality, his tent was largely symbolic. He was making his Bedouin origins clear to the world.

Life in the Bedouin Tent

The Bedouin tent is an infinitely mobile structure, ruled in co-operation by its father figure and his wife. It should be clear that without a wife the father has no tent – the father is then, in effect, rootless and homeless. I emphasise here that the father and the wife are an essential co-operative unit.

When it is pitched and functioning, the tent is divided by a curtain, closed when visitors are there but often open. Behind it is the third of the tent space which is occupied by women. Men do not enter that space and most of the women keep out of the two-thirds reserved for the men. The wife may sometimes be seen there when precious resources or marriage or the like are discussed, and she or one of her daughters fetch and carry for the males, a job performed by children in the main. The marital mat or carpet, on which the father and the wife sleep when he is present or so inclined, and on which the children are conceived and born, is placed in the male side of the tent.

Children, young boys and girls use the women's third the tent and play there without let or hindrance. Later, boy children begin to sit on the dividing line between the two sections and absorb the ways of the men as part of the masculine education.

Between men and women there is a clear division of labour. Women weave the material for the tent from wool given to them by the males. They pitch and strike the tent and make the necessary adjustments for wind and weather. Women collect kindling and water. They milk the sheep, goats, cattle or camels.

Males, who are old enough, are herdsmen and shepherds. They also cultivate the arable lands and deal with the storage of grain. When time is right, bands of young men, dressed in women's clothes for the occasion, travel round their territory shearing the sheep. They are allowed some licence to sing, something they would never otherwise do in the vicinity of the tents.

The fathers decide when and where the tent will move, when their progeny will marry and to whom. The men and the women of the tent do not eat together, nor do they have legitimate demands on each other's time. Men, therefore, are free of the duty of spending what we now call quality time with their spouses.

Boy children go through a slow progression into manhood, being at first given a few sheep or goats to tend but staying near the tents. As they grow older, they are trusted with larger flocks or herds further from their abode. Eventually they are allowed to herd camels, the most difficult work a man can do for these animals wander widely after food and have a tendency to get lost.

Boys cannot marry until their father permits them to do so. That may take a long time, for the loss of labour and the cost of the marriage can be an unwanted call on his resources. This leads to frustration, especially as premarital sex is not, overtly anyway, permitted. Once a son is married, he will have a tent of his own and, when children appear, he will, at last, have achieved personal independence within the tribe.

Once the father has been persuaded to let his son marry he will open negations about the bride price. This is calculated in resources, such as camels, sheep or cattle, and has much to do with the status of the bride and groom's family. The preferred marriage partner is a cousin of the appropriate age, in which case the bride price is generally small. If the bride is from another section of the tribe, or a client tribe, the price can be greater. The whole of the bride price is not paid immediately and a good portion of it is often left outstanding as an obligation or debt, a means of binding families together and one reason why obligations are complex. The groom himself purchases necklaces, wristlets and anklets, as well as pots and pans, for his bride. This becomes her property when she is married. This is separate from the bride price.

The way power was exercised amongst the Bedouin is not easy to describe. Western observers too easily ascribed more power to sheikhs than they actually had. It is convenient but its dangers are obvious. However, it helps to understand Gaddafi.

In the 1950s, the tribes appeared to be egalitarian at first sight. People dressed similarly, whatever their status. However, the sheikh's tent was always largest. His horse was often tethered close at hand. The best sheikhs had the best horses. Mobility was important as he needed to attend gatherings over a wide area and move quickly to settle disputes. His herds were often the largest in the camp. His hospitality was the most generous. Visitors made for his tent to drink the sweet tea, which always appeared to be available. People gathered in the Sheikh's tent for discussions or to hear him recount his past achievements.

One of the most difficult concepts for the Western observer to grasp was the relationship between wealth and leadership amongst the Bedouin. The power of a sheikh did not derive from material wealth as it is understood in the West. It arose from a nebulous quality within him and what we now call networking. My conclusion is that he exercised a form of power which depended on a complex skein of kinship and personal relationships, and also on favours given and received. I must add that I also observed startling instances of ruthlessness, either exercised personally or by proxy. It was deployed on my behalf on two occasions. Perhaps these were uncommon, but I suspect not.[5]

Nasser the Hero

When Muammar Gaddafi was young, Gamal Abdul Nasser held sway Egypt and his propaganda was spread by radio across the Libyan Desert, and by Egyptian teachers in Libyan schools. It should surprise no one that Nasser was Gaddafi's hero. Ahmad Said, the head of Nasser's radio station, the 'Voice of the Arabs', was the voice that the young men of the tribes listened to with notable results. Gaddafi could hardly have escaped his unscrupulous but brilliant propaganda. It was virulently anti-colonial and notably anti-British. There were reasons for this.

Britain had acquired an extensive empire in the Middle East after the Turks had been beaten in the Great War, and Nasser's role in its demise was pivotal. When Nasser first came to public attention in 1952, Fiasal II was King of Iraq and his cousin Hussain was King of Jordan. King Hussain's army was commanded by the British officer known as Glub Pasha. Jordan's king in the making, who was to succeed to the throne at the age of 17, was still at Harrow.

Aden was a British base, though its hinterland was never really pacified. It did, however, dominate that nest of vipers known as Somalia. The Sudan was shared, as it were, with Egypt and was largely ruled by a few Oxbridge graduates. Bahrain, the Trucal and Oman states, Kuwait and the rest were sympathetic to Britain in one way or another. Most of all, the Canal Zone was a British base of enormous importance in the maintenance of power in the region as the Suez Canal dominated the movement of shipping to and from the Far East.

Not only was shipping thus controlled, but the British Royal Air Force had unquestioned air passage over all these strategically crucial countries, enabling it to maintain its military 'Air Bridge' with its possessions in the Far East. It could, or rather appeared to, maintain air superiority over the southwestern borders of the Soviet Empire.

Institutions such as the British Bank of the Middle East and Barclays DCO handled much of the money and British Petroleum kept its eye on most of the oil. The Egyptian army was supplied with what Bevin, a British Labour Foreign Minister, once notably called rubbish.

That someone should defy all that military power seemed inconceivable. Gamal Adbul Nasser did just that. He was a tall, rather shy Egyptian army officer, born in Alexandria in 1918. His father, a Post Office clerk with poor fellaheen roots, had only attended a local primary school, but his determination to make his way in the world greatly influenced his son.

Gamal Abdul Nasser was a determined student and obtained his primary and secondary school leaving certificates. He was also politically active and led anti-British demonstrations. His tenacity and diligence at secondary school, and his virulently anti-British activity, was to be echoed by Gaddafi.

Nasser was accepted into the Egyptian Military Academy in 1937, together with most of those who were to form a group called the Free Officers, who were to be Nasser's power base in the future. The military academy had been exclusive to the sons of beys and pashas, but it opened its doors to cadets with secondary school leaving certificates and leadership potential. Most of Nasser's Free Officers had also benefited from this change in selection policy. As a cadet, Nasser was a voracious reader of history, politics and biography. Gaddafi has often stated that he too read widely.

The immediate aims of the revolutionary movement Nasser was to lead were thus developed after considerable research by a man of great intelligence and immense mental energy. These aims were neither Marxist nor Islamist, but fervently nationalistic.

Nasser was determined to overthrow the Egyptian monarchy, then personified by the sybaritic King Farouk. He was also determined to remove the British military occupation of his country and to redistribute to the fellaheen the fertile land which was mostly in the hands of a few landowners. For his part, Gaddafi was to remove King Idris, get rid of the British and US military bases from Libya and break the hold of the big oil companies on the only real source of wealth in his otherwise impoverished homeland.

Nasser's chance came when King Farouk's Wafadist Party government was in some political trouble. It had decided that an anti-British stance would ensure support, so it abrogated the Anglo-Egyptian treaty, arranged for the 30,000 civilian workers to leave the British army in the lurch in the Canal Zone and encouraged sabotage and terrorist attacks on British military establishments. This had the effect of neutralising the strategic value of the Canal Zone because the British military effort was taken up in compensating for the loss of Egyptian labour and in self-defence.

Predictably, the British failed to appreciate the situation. Riots broke out in Cairo and many British-owned properties and iconic buildings were attacked and torched, including the famous Shepherd's Hotel. This incident sounded the death knell for King Farouk and his government, and the Free Officers, nominally headed by the distinguished General Muhammad Neguib, decided to seize power in 1952. The British, who were not enamoured of Farouk and his government, were probably lulled into a sense of security by Neguib and did nothing to intervene. This was to be another strange parallel with the unexpected failure of the British to intervene in Gaddafi's coup in Libya.

The Egyptian Free Officers formed a Revolutionary Command Council with Neguib as its chairman and set about consolidating their power. By the end of 1954, Nasser had removed Neguib and was in undisputed control of Egypt. That year he published a book called *The Philosophy of Revolution*. Once again we can draw parallels with Gaddafi and his Revolutionary Command Council in Libya and his publication of *The Green Book*. By 31 March 1956, Nasser had successfully removed the British from the Canal Zone.

The affair of the Aswan Dam, which Nasser wanted to build across the Nile to produce hydroelectricity to underpin his development plans, was to shock the Arab world. Nasser had hoped to finance it with loans from the USA and Britain. The loans were refused. Nasser was incensed and he decided on a bold stroke. He nationalised the Suez Canal.

The British prime minister, Anthony Eden, launched an Anglo-French invasion of Egypt. On 5 November 1957, the British, with French support, landed in Suez, and one of the most ignominious campaigns fought by the British for a number of years commenced. Eden, ill with prostate trouble, became obsessed with Nasser. The USA was not amused and put irresistible pressure on the British to withdraw, as did some Commonwealth governments. Russia joined in with the condemnation and the British forces were withdrawn without honour. For Libya the situation was fraught, but in much of the Arab world the humiliation of the British was received with acclamation.

However, the children of the Libyan tents and the towns listened to Umm Kalthoum, the Egyptian singer, the most famous of her time, and dubbed the opium of the Arabs. Her songs, some of which could last for two hours, drew audiences from all over the Arab-speaking world to the 'Voice of the Arabs' and Nasser's propaganda. She died in her late 70s in February 1975. I suggest that the effect on Gaddafi of Umm Kalthoum and Ahmad Said were profound and would account for his naive but virulent anti-colonial and anti-British stance.

The propaganda broadcasts were delivered in classical Arabic, the powerful influence of which is not well understood in the West. Since Gaddafi has exhibited some of the traits of one who is carried away by language, often his own, it is worth quoting H.A.R. Gibb in his *Modern Trends in Islam*: '... upon the Arab mind the impact of artistic speech is immediate; the words, passing through no filter of logic or reflection which might weaken them or deaden their effect, go straight to the head.' Perhaps we might widen this to include Gaddafi's long, rambling speeches.

The Friendly Occupation

In his interview with Professor Jouve on 2 November 2002, Gaddafi was asked what his thoughts were as a young man. He stated that his country was occupied by foreign forces. There were, he said, five American military bases and the same number of British military bases. Whilst this was not strictly accurate, it is clear that the friendly occupation by the British and Americans was objectionable to him and probably his co-conspirators. It is important, therefore, to understand the feelings engendered by the presence of the British and US military bases on Libyan soil.

The main US military presence was the large USAF base called Wheelus Field on the coast near Tripoli. Its strategic value was as a staging post for a potential US military engagement in the Middle East or India; otherwise it provided a training base for aircraft using a bombing range in the desert. Some of the USAF personnel lived in town and local Arab workers were employed for menial tasks on the base. USAF personnel were not encouraged to live on the local economy, which was perceived to be threatening. Mostly they preferred to live in married quarters on the base, ship their cars and household goods from the USA and buy their food and consumables at their own supermarket, the Post Exchange. Thus, whilst the base offered unskilled and menial employment to locals, the local businesses, with the exception of a few night-clubs perhaps, did not benefit greatly from their presence.

As Gaddafi said in a speech in Tripoli on 16 October 1969, soon after his successful coup: 'The Arab people of Libya … can no longer live side by side with the foreign bases … Nor will the [Libyan] armed forces … tolerate living in their shacks while the bases of imperialism exist on Libyan terri-tory.'[6] Many did live in shacks constructed from cardboard, wood and corrugated iron.

The British military bases were in a number of places, one of which was Bab Azzizia where Gaddafi was later to reside. The British military families lived in little colonies in town and in married quarters on the bases. It was probably for this reason that the British military maintained an exclusive beach club in a choice seaside suburb. There was also a NAAFI superstore in town which was exclusive to British military and diplo-matic personnel. As they did in India and now do in Spain, the British constructed little replicas of Britain in a hot climate.

Whatever the rationale, this was a de facto colonisation of the city of Tripoli and typically British in character. One thing that is remembered with anger by many of the people the British had colonised was that their clubs were exclusive to white British people – of the right class of course. Ask any old resident of Shanghai, Nairobi, Suva, Lahore, Rangoon or Accra to point out where the 'white man only' clubs were in the colonial days and they will do so with lingering resentment.

For the young Gaddafi, the hated legacy of the Italian colo-nial regime still flourished, especially in Tripoli. In 1958 it was still almost an Italian city and it intimidated the Bedouin, who felt unwelcome on its streets, and the dwellers in the shanty towns on its periphery, who laboured at menial tasks within it.

Israel, the Enemy that did not Exist

Nasser's propaganda from Cairo was full of anger about Israel, the visceral hatred of which existed in Libya when Gaddafi was young and has affected his foreign policy. Whilst time has done much to mute the hatred, it still exists and frequently finds expression. This is not the place to rehearse the complex history of the state of Israel, but to view it from the perspective of young Libyans, such as Gaddafi and his co-conspirators, in the 1960s. It was, in effect, a view of Israel reflected in the distorting mirror of Egyptian propaganda.

The history of the Holocaust was not understood by Libyans since they knew little or nothing about it, nor were they able to grasp the relevance of the Diaspora to the exiled Jewish populations. They were thus unable to see the pressing need for a Jewish homeland. For them, the Jordanian Arabs were the indigenous population of Palestine.

In essence, but probably a serious oversimplification, the British had held a mandate in Palestine since the Turks were defeated in the Great War and there had been a gradual influx of Jewish immigrants and a growth in violence perpetuated by Jewish underground forces, such as the Irgun, the Haganah and the Lehi. In 1945 President Truman endorsed the Zionist demand that 100,000 Jews should be allowed into Palestine.

The British now had to deal with a flood of Jewish illegal immigration on the one hand and a widespread campaign of violence by Zionists on the other. The violence culminated in July 1945, with the blowing up of the King David Hotel in Jerusalem, in which British government and military personnel were killed.

On 14 May 1948 the British mandate in Jordan ended and her troops withdrew. The same day the state of Israel was proclaimed and recognised by the USA. A war ensued when the regular forces of Transjordan, Syria, Iraq and Egypt entered Israel in support of the Palestine Arabs. The Israelis were better equipped and led than the Arabs and won. There was an exodus of Palestinians and the semi-desert region called the Gaza Strip, and an enclave on the west bank of the Jordan, filled with refugees.

The perceived harshness to the Arab inhabitants of Jordan left a legacy of bitterness against Israel, and the two Western powers most responsible for the creation of Israel – the USA and the UK. This has been the most powerful factor behind the growth of anti-Western feeling in the Arab world ever since.

In Libya, during the period I worked there, the hatred of Israel was profound. Officially Israel did not exist, so the emotion directed against it took the form of removing any mention of it from books, airline timetables and maps. No one who had been to Israel was permitted to enter Libya, nor were any goods that had been to Israel or were made there permitted entrance.

I have endeavoured to find an expression of the intense feelings about Israel that my Libyan colleagues expressed to me over a period of more than eight years. Their criticism was mostly expressed calmly. Often, however, anger spilt over. I once spent well over three hours before dawn attempting to release a commercial aircraft which was impounded because I could not prove it had never been to Israel.

These harsh words of Arnold Toynbee are close to the Libyan Arab view in the 1960s:

> Britain had control of Palestine for thirty years ... admitting year by year a quota of Jewish immigrants. The reason why the state of Israel exists today and why over 1,500,000 Palestine Arabs are refugees is that, for thirty years, Jewish immigration was imposed on the Palestine Arabs by British military power until the immigrants were sufficiently numerous and sufficiently well-armed to be able to fend for themselves with tanks and aircraft of their own ...[7]

Muammar Gaddafi Joins the Army and Plans a Coup

The closest I came to Gaddafi was in the 1960s through Ted Lough, the senior British army officer who commanded the British military mission to the Libyan army from 1960 to 1966. My diaries show that Ted had a number of British army officers and senior NCOs on his staff. At the time the Royal Libyan Army had about 5,000 officers and men on its nominal role. It had been formed, as I understood it, around a nucleus of Libyans who had served in Egypt during the Second World War in the Libyan Arab Force.

As part of his duties, Ted Lough played a prominent role in the Royal Libyan Military Academy, the fledgling Sandhurst or West Point of the Libyan army, which had been set up in 1957. I understood that officer cadets were then being recruited from young men with leadership qualities and a secondary school certificate of education. They were required to spend some time in the ranks before admission to the academy, an echo of the British system designed to ensure that candidates had sufficient physical and mental fitness to survive officer training.

This gave Gaddafi and some of his friends a unique opportunity to gain a commission, which they deliberately exploited. In the past commissions had been given to the sons of powerful tribal and aristocratic families. Of this Gaddafi stated: '... several of my fellow revolutionaries studied with me. When we decided to go to the Academy, it was not because we wanted to become professional soldiers but because we wanted to infiltrate the institution and prepare for revolution.'[8]

Gaddafi's records show that he was admitted to the seventh intake of officer cadets. Ted Lough appears to have found him to be very difficult indeed. One reason, some suggest, is that he refused to learn or use English properly, thus making it very difficult for Ted's instructors to teach him. I believe that Gaddafi was re-coursed at least once and that Ted tried to have him removed a few times.

In an interview with David Blundy and Andrew Lycett, Ted is quoted as saying: 'He was the most backward of cadets. He did twice as long as the other cadets in the Benghazi Academy; 98 per cent of the cadets passed, 2 per cent failed, and he was one of them.' Ted was not aware that success in the army was not Gaddafi's main aim.

Ted did not like him because he was rude to his British instructors. Blundy and Lycett suggest that Gaddafi may have been protected by the Libyan commander-in-chief in Benghazi. He must surely have been protected in some way, but trying to attribute Gaddafi's luck to some deep conspiracy is often a waste of time. It has to be said that there was a severe case of administrative lethargy in Libya in those days. He is more likely, in my view, to have survived because no one bothered to make a decision.[9]

Whilst Blundy and Lycett do not emphasise the point, Gaddafi's rudeness to the British officers and men was part of his plan. It made him a hero and is consistent with his behaviour throughout his career. Time and again observers have described this trait, which has not endeared him to Arab or Western statesmen. As Dirk Vandewalle wrote in his admirable *History of Libya*, 'He attacked both friends and foe alike with a sense of righteousness that antagonised his closest partners in the region and beyond as much as his enemies'.[10]

Ted Lough thought Gaddafi was cruel. This has also been a consistent facet of his behaviour and had the effect of strengthening his hand in Libya. I was told that Ted had written notes to the British diplomats in Tripoli and Benghazi, warning them about a disturbing trend amongst younger Libyan army officers. Ted and his staff had been uneasy about them for some time. In particular, he is alleged to have reported an incident on the firing ranges when a Libyan officer shot one of his colleagues. The shooting was cruel, deliberate and observed with relish by the friends of the perpetrator, who is said by some to have been Gaddafi. Ted passed the news on to the British Embassy for the MI6 employees to ponder. The British maintained a growing file on possible conspirators and had been anticipating some sort of coup against King Idris but had been watching the wrong man, as had the Egyptians, who were busy trying to extend their influence over the Libyan oil fields. That is probably why both parties were surprised when Gaddafi and his young friends suddenly seized power.

In preparing their military coup, Gaddafi and his fellow cadets at the Royal Libyan Military Academy in Benghazi must have spent a great deal of their free time sounding out friends and foes and making plans. His core group was called the Free Officers Movement, as had been Nasser's conspirators in the Egyptian army. The loyalty of each of his early conspirators was assured because they had joined the army for the express purpose of mounting a coup. It should be remembered that Gaddafi began to foment a coup whilst at school. Apart from Nasser, there are few heads of state who can claim this distinction. Until he gained power, Gaddafi knew nothing but conspiracy. He wielded power as though he had been engaged in a worldwide conspiracy for forty-two years.

Let us first look at the early problems facing Gaddafi and his companions as they plotted their way to power in Libya. It is easier for senior officers who command key units to organise a coup. In Libya it would not have been too difficult for the army chief of staff, Aziz al Shelhi, to seize power in this way, and there is ample evidence that he was planning to do so. It was an entirely different matter for army officer cadets barely out of their teens to plan to do so, but this is what happened.

Between entering the academy in 1961 and executing the coup on 1 September 1969, the core group, in this case the Free Officers, had to meet regularly without arousing suspicion. This was more easily achieved within the military academy but harder when the conspirators were commissioned and posted to different units. In Gaddafi's case, he was not completely successful. There is room to suspect that the murder in 1963 of the Libyan commander of the Royal Military Academy was carried out because he suspected Gaddafi and his fellow cadets. He would have had to have been very bad at his job to have missed what was going on.

Expanding a conspiracy in a disciplined army is best achieved using the cell system. That is, each officer of the core group forms his own cell into which he recruits loyal members. Each cell communicates with the others only through the leader. A careful assessment of officers outside the conspiracy has to be made to make judgements on the possible reaction of each military unit. Potential threats need eliminating, without drawing too much suspicion to the conspirators. The king made it easy for Gaddafi by leaving the country. The Crown prince, the diwan, the army chief of staff and a number of powerful civilians would have been earmarked for arrest.

Once the loyalty of each conspirator has been assured, placing them in key posts takes time. The major threat to Gaddafi was the king's loyal and elite Cyrenaican Defence Force. He may have neutralised that threat by recruiting a key young CIDEF officer into one of the cells. He may have done the same with the Tripolitanian Defence Force, which posed a lesser but still significant threat.

Communication plays a central role in a coup. To subvert the military communication network was Gaddafi's top priority. Once that was established, the conspirators were in a position to read all signal traffic, to shut down communication between commanders or send orders and instructions as though they came from commanders.

After he was commissioned, Gaddafi specialised in signals. He was sent to Britain on a course with the British Royal Armoured Corps at Bovingdon. He also underwent military training in Greece.

According to members of the British military mission in Libya, Gaddafi subsequently took over the main Libyan army signals centre in Benghazi, for which he ordered advanced equipment.[11] It is clear that Gaddafi was able to communicate with any Libyan army unit he wished and also control the codes and ciphers.

The number of plots increased as the king's grasp on power waned and the confusion played into Gaddafi's hands. On 1 September 1969, the BBC reported:

King Idris of Libya has been deposed in what appears to have been a bloodless coup. A group of military officers have seized power and declared the country a republic. But the king, who is in Turkey, has dismissed the coup as 'unimportant'. According to reports from the capital, Tripoli, troops and tanks converged on the city in the early hours of the morning. Within two hours they had taken key positions and the royal palace, military and security headquarters were surrounded by 0500. All communications with the outside world were cut and a curfew was imposed.

9

Gaddafi II
The Pariah State and Human Rights Issues

We now feel certain that Gaddafi's secret police formed a state within a state, as did the Cheka and its successors in the USSR and the Stasi in East Germany. Each of these secret pseudo-states reflected the national characteristics of their country of origin. Libya created a secret police state which was managed by the tribal family of Muammar Gaddafi.

Severe international sanctions imposed on Gaddafi's regime in 1989 and the consequent impoverishment of the people created the conditions in which Islamist guerrillas could gain the ear of the malcontents. In the early 1990s, the Libyan Islamic Fighting Group was formed from Jihadists returning from the Afghan war with Russia. This group aimed to replace Gaddafi's regime with an Islamist state with the strict implementation of Sharia law. There was an attempt by this group on Gaddafi's life, an event that reinforced his self-preservation policies.

On 1 September 1969, Gaddafi seized power during a period of unusual unrest in Libya, caused by events outside the country, which he was able to exploit by developing a national paranoia directed against the British, the USA and Israel. His coup was bloodless because he was the quickest to act during the power vacuum left by the departure and abdication of King Idris.

He took over a state that was earning enough revenue from oil to allow him unique powers of patronage, the ability to purchase the support of the small population, acquire huge stocks of modern armaments and indulge in grandiose schemes. It soon became clear that he had unprecedented personal power, which he was able to wield without any let or hindrance other than the limitations of his intellect and experience.

Perhaps the young revolutionaries came to power in a bloodless coup because the army was not sure who was leading it. The immediate seat of power in the few days that followed the coup lay in the self-proclaimed Revolutionary Command Council, an echo of that which Nasser had created in Egypt after his coup. The RCC immediately declared that Libya was now a republic, warned other revolutionaries off with dire threats and attempted to assure foreign governments.

One potentially crucial event that did not happen was the intervention of the paramilitary Cyrenaican Defence Force. Gaddafi may have won them over. They were close to the king and, like him, may have realised that there was no advantage in opposing the coup.

There was a pause whilst the RCC consolidated its hold by putting the Crown prince under house arrest and also arresting some senior army officers and government officials who might have opposed it.

On 7 September 1969, the day that the USA officially recognised the new Libyan government, the RCC announced that it had appointed a government. An American-educated technician, Mahmud Sulayman al Maghrabi, was appointed as prime minister. He had been a political prisoner since 1967. A council of eight ministers was also appointed, of which two were military officers. The council was instructed to implement the state's general policy, as drawn up by the RCC.

On 8 September, the RCC promoted Captain Muammar Gaddafi to the rank of colonel and appointed him commander-in-chief of the Libyan armed forces.

It is legitimate to ask why the coup was unopposed. Why, for example, did Britain not intervene? The ease with which a group of junior army officers succeeded in their coup still arouses questions in those quarters where accusations of American or British connivance stem from anti-Western sentiment.

As to the possibility of American connivance in the coup, I have no real insights, but their embassy in Libya was between ambassadors at the time. Ronald Bruce St John, who is a very reliable historian, suggests that the USA had no information on the Gaddafi group. He quotes others when he states that the USA did supply the RCC with information about budding counter-coups on one occasion at least and probably more.[1]

It is clear that the British expected a coup and were pre-pared to make the best of it when it came. It had been the British policy to train the Libyan army and cosset it with support from the British military mission, in the hope that a military coup would rebound in their favour. Though they had the warnings of Ted Lough on file, they had not expected Gaddafi to prevail over Aziz al Shelhi, nor had the Egyptians who had also cultivated al Shelhi's favour.

Did Britain support Gaddafi's coup? It is most unlikely. Whilst in Libya, I was required to meet a number of British government ministers who passed through Idris and Benina airports on their way to sell arms or negotiate an orderly withdrawal from a colony. One was on his way to Aden, from whence the British were withdrawing after some unpleasant events. The minister and his team were positively unimpres-sive. The story is relevant because Britain was rolling up her empire. The loss of India, the Malayan troubles, the Suez deba-cle, the Mau Mau in Kenya, the rebels in the Radfan in the heartland of Aden, EOKA in Cyprus and more of the same had accumulated to sap British self-belief and reduce the sup-port for imperialist adventures.

A sad little home-bound trickle of retiring British colonial governors passing through the Libyan airports was followed by a flush of new heads of state bound for the United Nations in New York or to meet the queen in London. Presidents of newly independent countries, such as Jomo Kenyatta of Kenya, Kwame N'Khrumah of Ghana and Dom Mintoff of Malta required my attendance as they stretched legs whilst their aircraft refuelled. The old order was changing at an ever-increasing rate.

Some of the new heads of state had been imprisoned by the British at one time or other in their careers or had led long struggles for independence, or both. That was not the case in Libya. However, the new regime presented itself as revolution-ary and, in common with others of that ilk, needed an enemy to confront. It was to find one in the unwitting British.

It was soon clear that the British hope of gaining influence by training the Libyan army was a misjudgement. The trainees learnt quickly that power came out the barrel of a gun. Many of the military coups that took place in the old empire after independence were led by men trained in British military schools and staff colleges, but their regimes had no intention of accepting British influence. This was the case in Libya.

The British Labour politician Dennis Healey was the British Minister of Defence between 1964 and 1970. He visited Libya in that capacity to sell arms to the government of King Idris. His recollections about Gaddafi's coup are interesting:

> I also paid several visits to Libya … It was obvious that the monarchy was about to fall at any moment to an army coup, and I tried to guess which of the young colonels I met was most likely to lead it. I decided it would probably be Colonel Shelhi … I was wrong.

He also wrote: 'I was told by our Ambassador … that Shelhi had been woken by his batman on the morning off the coup with the words: Excuse me sir, the Revolution has begun. Don't be silly, was the reply. It's tomorrow.'[2]

The upshot is that all parties expected a military coup. They decided to make the best of it and to wait and see how the RCC played its hand. Ted Lough apart, no diplomat or MI6 or CIA agent could have predicted the Gaddafi phenomenon.

There may have been some misgiving when the RCC asserted that engaging in political activity was treasonable and that the RCC was the unchallengeable highest authority in the Libyan Arab Republic. Trade unions were made illegal and supporters of King Idris and his regime were tried in courts presided over by RCC members. There were some puritanical measures, such as closing the nightclubs, where show girls were required to make conversation with male guests, and banning the sale of alcoholic beverages, thus creating a thriving private home-brewing culture amongst expatriate workers. It must have been something of a sacrifice to one member of the RCC, Major Jalloud, who was known to have enjoyed the company of women and the comfort of bourbon whilst training in the USA.

There now came at least two attempts to bring the regime down. One was said to have been initiated by Omar al Shelhi, now in exile, who attempted to hire a company called Watch Guard, a group of British mercenary soldiers run by David

Stirling, the British war hero and founder of the SAS. The idea was that a contingent of SAS men should raid Tripoli and release a number of political prisoners, including Aziz al Shelhi, from jail. The British mercenaries were then to withdraw and leave the prisoners, and others, to mount a counter-coup. The operation has been described in detail in a book called *The Hilton Assignment*. The jail was notoriously awful and was cynically called the Tripoli Hilton.

Stirling, who was well connected in influential circles in Britain, was quietly but firmly warned off. There were two further attempts to revive the operation with French mercenaries, both of which were betrayed by Western intelligence services and stopped by diplomatic intervention.

It appeared that some of David Stirling's associates were convinced that the counter-coup would succeed. I suspect that their optimism was ill founded. That Stirling was quietly warned off is sometimes cited to prove that Gaddafi was supported by the British. It is more likely that the British government did not wish to deal with the diplomatic fallout from a counter-coup financed by Omar al Shelhi and involving a prominent war hero, especially as it was unlikely to succeed.

There was another over-ambitious attempted counter-coup planned by a relative of King Idris, Prince Abdulla Abed, a colourful personage known as the Black Prince. He was said to have funded a force of mercenaries recruited in Chad, with the intention of ousting Gaddafi. If it got further than an aspiration, I would be surprised. However, in the event, the French got wind of it and managed to alert the RCC. The French were later to make some spectacular armaments deals with the Gaddafi regime.

The case of the ex-SAS officer and mercenary, Simon Mann, and his failed attempt to overthrow the government of President Teodoro Obiang Nguema Mbasogo in Equatorial Guinea in 2004, is a sufficient lesson. The Mann operation, in which he was caught and jailed, implicated Sir Mark Thatcher, bringing his mother, Lady Thatcher, some embarrassment by association. These sorts of heroics are best confined to fiction.

The Libyan RCC began to develop a personality cult around Gaddafi and to strengthen their hand in Libya with a series of gestures. It seems to have concluded that oil revenues were sufficient to compensate for the loss of aid and rents received for the US and British military bases. They also gambled that Britain and the US would acquiesce to the early removal of their military, providing they continued to receive favourable treatment for their oil companies. Gaddafi now made a number of public speeches and staged events which led the Libyan people to believe that he was confronting the imperialist enemies and removing them.

One of his famous gestures was to attempt to drive through the USAF base at Wheelus. Air Force General Daniel 'Chappie' James had assumed command of Wheelus Air Force Base after the coup. He later wrote in his memoirs:

> One day Khadafy ran a column of half-tracks through my base, right through the housing area at full speed. I shut the barrier down at the gate and met Khadafy a few yards outside it. He had a fancy gun and a holster and kept his hand on it. I had my .45 in my belt. I told him to move his hand away. If he had pulled that gun, he never would have cleared his holster. They never sent any more half-tracks.

Gaddafi was to make much of this incident in his speeches when he complained that the gate of Wheelus Field had been shut against him.[3]

The gestures were mainly for a Libyan audience, because both Britain and the USA readily agreed to relinquish their bases by early 1970, but Gaddafi made sure that he was seen as an anti-imperialist hero by declaring the anniversaries of their evacuations as public holidays.

Gaddafi struck two further blows against the British by nationalising Barclays Dominion, Colonial and Overseas Bank and cancelling arms contracts of some considerable value made by the previous regime with British companies.

Taming the Oil Companies

Gaddafi had learnt a lesson in brinkmanship from Nasser, who had defied British might by nationalising the Suez Canal. He would apply it when dealing with the oil companies. He set out to break the hold of the Seven Sisters' cartel and assert the sovereignty of Libya over its own oil. In doing so, he changed the geopolitics of oil forever. This was an achievement of considerable importance to other oil producers, but also had the effect of greatly increasing the price of oil worldwide.

He opened his campaign by employing Abdullah Tariki as his oil advisor. Tariki had been oil minister in Saudi Arabia but was sacked for opposing the Seven Sisters, who monopolised Saudi oil concessions through a single consortium called Aramco. They could, if they wished, shut the country down, like Iran in the 1950s. Libya was the only oil-producing country in the Middle East in which the Seven Sisters did not have a monopoly, because of the independents such as Bunker Hunt and Occidental.

The independent with the largest and richest field was Occidental. It was vulnerable to attack because its only source of oil was Libya, it was in debt to Bechtel, the company that had built its crude-oil pipeline, and it had won its concession as a result of a notorious sweetener.

Gaddafi's first move was to confiscate the concession of a small independent called Chappaqua, on the grounds that it had been obtained by bribery. This sent a clear message that the new regime had found incriminating evidence. It had charged Omar al Shelhi with corruption in absentia and it was said that Occidental had dealings with him. My erstwhile neighbour George Williamson, by this time Occidental's man in Libya, told Edward J. Epstein that the regime had subpoenaed all Occidental's documents in Tripoli and had found evidence of bribery.

Williamson also told Epstein that Gaddafi's next move came on 3 June 1970. It was to cut Occidental's permitted oil production by nearly 40 per cent, with a further 10 per cent cut to come in August. The final threat was to nationalise Occidental on 1 September 1970, on the first anniversary of the revolution. This was a series of crushing blows, which brought Armand Hammer, the company's owner, to Libya to deal directly with Major Jalloud, the second in command of the RCC. Jalloud was competent and well briefed about the oil business. He was a formidable negotiator well known to George Williamson.

On 1 September 1970, Armand Hammer signed an agreement which allowed Libya to have 55 per cent of Occidental's oil exports and power over the future pricing of its oil. Within weeks all the other oil companies operating in Libya had signed a similar agreement. Once they had acceded to Libya's demands, other oil-producing countries put pressure on them and achieved similar agreements. The Organisation of Oil-Producing Companies began to wield much more power and the price of oil was to rise inexorably.[4]

Gaddafi now made it clear that he intended to use oil as a political weapon against Israel. Negotiating on behalf of Libya, Algeria, Iraq and Saudi Arabia, Gaddafi declared that they, and not foreign companies, would set the price of oil flowing into Europe. In 1971 Libya also nationalised BP's oil concessions, including the Sarir field shared with Bunker Hunt. In addition, Gaddafi withdrew Libya's sterling balances in London, a move that he associated with Britain's failure to stop Iran occupying the three strategic islands off Abu Musa in the Persian Gulf in the face of Arab opposition, thus making it clear that he was wielding the oil weapon on behalf of wider Arab interests. The oil companies began to lose confidence in Libya but the Western governments failed to change their relationship with Israel.

The international community had begun to take notice when Gaddafi started to use oil as a weapon against Israel, which he saw as an instrument of Western imperialism. It was slower to take note of the inexorable growth of human rights violations within Libya. These violations grew out of the attempt to impose the 1 September revolution on the people from the top.

The Green Book and the Green Terror

Gaddafi and his fellows first espoused a brand of socialism, partly borrowed from Nasser's early days and partly indigenous, in that it was influenced by five Bedouin tribal customs. The first requirement is that land and water resources are corporately owned by the tribe. The second is that each family unit has its own tent. The third is that the access to decision making is available to all adult males in the forum of the tent. The fourth is that the tribe provides its members with collective protection and security, and the fifth is that the sheikh exercises power, or, as Gaddafi himself put it in his *Green Book*, those who are strongest in society hold the reins of government.[5]

Gaddafi's first attempt to mobilise some revolutionary zeal and bring his version of socialism to the Libyan people with public rallies, state-sponsored demonstrations and marches brought only ephemeral responses from a people preoccupied with family, clan, tribe and the business of earning a living.

What pleased the people, though, were the regime's efforts to improve medical care, housing, infrastructure, education and social care, much of which was done in the first flush of power. Also, the new regime was to make the abandoned Italian colonial land available to new farmers and cultivators at a fraction of its real value. This was well received, as were the good start-up loans available.

It is worth remembering that the old problem of lack of technical, medical and industrial capability was still acute. In the early days of the new regime, the Egyptians provided much of the expertise. The growing dependence on the USSR for military hardware and medical help brought a number of expatriates from the Soviet bloc to work in Libya.

Gaddafi concluded that the government bureaucracy and the tribal structure were too conservative and were holding back his revolution so, in 1971, he brought into being the Arab Socialist Union, based on a similar organisation that Nasser had set up, unsuccessfully, in Egypt. This was his attempt to impose socialism from the top down.

The Libyan version of the ASU held its first national congress in March and April 1972. The ASU failed to mobilise popular enthusiasm, but succeeded in splitting the RCC on Gaddafi's personal power and issues arising from his huge spending on armaments.

Serious student unrest and general discord promoted a brutal response in the form of the Green Terror, which, during 1973, saw the arrest of political opponents to the regime.

The arrival of a team of advisors from the East German Stasi signalled a new level of sophistication within the burgeoning security apparatus. The team was headed by the mysterious

Arabist Karl Hans, who was close to the notorious Karlo Wolf, the head of East Germany's intelligence services.

The most telling event occurred in 1973, when some members of the RCC, led by Omar Meheishi, attempted a coup which was supported by some army units. It failed and 200 senior army officers thought to have been involved were arrested. Meheishi escaped into exile, from where he was returned and brutally killed by Gaddafi's henchmen. In his brief exile, Meheishi had been joined by Major Abdul Moneim al Houni, who escaped the attentions of the enforcers.

The troubles that preceded and followed the split in the RCC led to the expulsion of Egyptian and Tunisian nationals and the arrest of two more of Gaddafi's erstwhile Free Officer colleagues, Mohammed Najm and Mukhtar Gerwi.

Gaddafi, having by now gathered more power into his own hands, turned his full attention to protecting his personal regime and embarked on a paradoxical policy of severe repression and popular empowerment.

Gaddafi was to develop the concept of an Armed People. From the mid-1970s he commenced military training in schools for 13 to 17-year-old students, followed by military service for all 18 to 35-year olds, active short military training for 35 to 45-year olds, and for 45 to 55-year olds he created a People's Militia to protect buildings in case of attacks. At the height of Muammar Gaddafi's power, it is likely that Libya was a near equal to some of the very heavily regulated societies, such as North Korea, in the number of people involved in its security and control apparatus.

The management and control of the extensive state military, security and intelligence network was concentrated in the hands of Gaddafi's blood relatives; relatives of his second wife, Safia Farkash; and members of his own tribe and two tribes allied to it, the Warfella of south-east Tripolitania and the Maqarah, the dominant tribe of the Fezzan. However, some young army officers from the Warfella tribe attempted a coup against Gaddafi in 1993, straining the tribe's relationship with him significantly. It was led by Colonels Muftah Gharum, Mustafa Balquasim Masud and Saad Salim Faraj, and was quelled by security forces and revolutionary guards.

The management of the secret services was in the hands of the Intelligence Bureau of the Leader. This was situated in the Bab Azzizia complex in Tripoli, alongside Gaddafi's residence. All other security organisations reported directly to this bureau and thus to Gaddafi.

The Jamahiriya Security Organisation, thought to have been headed by the ultra Gaddafi loyalist Abdulla al Senussi at one time, was the key secret service organisation with internal and international branches. The other key security organisation was the Military Secret Service based in Tripoli.

Security battalions, carefully recruited, well equipped and trained, were military units outside the army structure. They were largely in Gaddafi family hands. One such was the 32nd Reinforced Brigade of the Armed People and was one of three regime protection units, which together had a reported total strength of 10,000 men. The 32nd was commanded by Kamis Gaddafi, one of Muammar Gaddafi's sons, and was thus called the Kamis Brigade.

It is not unreasonable to state that Gaddafi and his regime remained in power for so long because he had ultimate and unlimited personal control of the intelligence-gathering and operational arms of a very large system of informants and enforcers, pervading every aspect of civilian and military life, including the police, the press and academia. There are some who argue that he rewrote history to lend support to his propaganda.[6]

The comprehensive nature, flexibility and effectiveness of Gaddafi's security system was demonstrated by the challenges it helped him withstand. It crushed attempted coups in 1973 and 1993, survived the effects of international sanctions between 1992 and 1999, suppressed Islamist revolts between 1995 and 1998 and thwarted attempts on the life of Gaddafi himself in 1998. It kept the population relatively docile during the frustrating period of inefficient centrally planned economy, where goods were only available from state supermarkets, and also during a war in neighbouring Chad, in which the Libyans were defeated.

Its evolution followed Gaddafi's proclamation of 2 March 1977, in which he began to develop his concept of a Jamahiriya, a word of complex meaning but which may be translated as a State of the People's Masses. The concept was explained in Gaddafi's *Green Book*, published in 1975–76, which 'shows the Masses the way to direct democracy ... based on the Third

Universal Theory'. This stated, in effect, that the Libyan people were divided into eighty-four Basic People's Congresses and forty-seven Municipal People's Congresses, to which every adult belonged. The legislative Basic People's Congresses selected and established executive People's Committees, which now replaced government administration.

The Basic People's Congresses and the People's Committees formed secretariats mandated to carry local resolutions to a General People's Congress of 1,000 members. Here the resolutions were to be debated, co-ordinated and sometimes implemented. According to *The Green Book*, the General People's Congress was said to be a 'gathering together of People's Congresses and People's Conferences'.

The General People's Congress, the legislative arm, elected and appointed a General People's Committee, which was effectively its executive or, to use a Western term, its Cabinet.

The Third Universal Theory thus abolished political parties and, theoretically, gave power, wealth and arms into the hands of the people. In this way the state also appeared to be abolished and became the State of the Masses.

The people were to be guided by the distillation of Gaddafi's mind as published in his naive little *Green Book*, in which his theories about government, religion, morality, family, property and the role of women are to be found.

The idealism of the Third Universal Theory and the State of the Masses was doomed by the enemies of democracy, apathy and bureaucracy. In Libya these ills were exacerbated by the huge distances people were required to travel to attend the various conferences. They too quickly became talking shops which were poorly attended and easy prey to those who wrote the agenda. Frustration occurred and local issues were constantly raised but rarely resolved. In practice, the power of the conferences were limited. They had no control over the oil industry, the armed forces and security services or, in practice, foreign policy. Oil paid for everything and so they were never required to raise money by taxation.

Independent of the People's Congresses, Gaddafi used the oil revenues to undertake a number of grandiose schemes. Oil refiners, the Misurata steel complex, a huge telescope and the 'Great Man Made River' project are notable examples. The

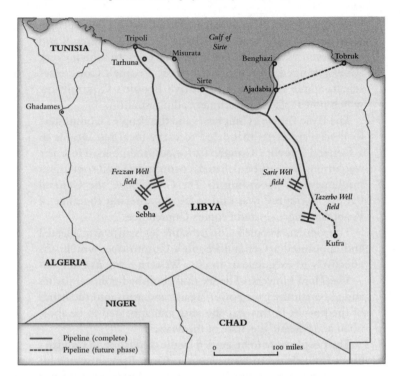

The 'Great Man Made River'. It is said to be the largest engineering undertaking in the world. It should provide half a million cubic metres of fossil water per day from the Nubian sandstone aquifer system to Libya's coastal settlements.

Great Man Made River was created to supply water to the burgeoning coastal cities and to supply a planned agricultural revolution. Even so, this source of water may yet prove to be a limiting factor in Libya in the long run.

The Great Man Made River was begun in 1991 and was said to be the largest engineering undertaking in the world. It was a twenty-five-year project designed to provide half a million cubic metres of water per day to Libya's coastal settlements through a network of concrete pipes totalling over 3,500km. It was one of the most lauded, and in some ways most worrying, hydrological engineering schemes, which arose out of the search for oil in Libya. It is laudable because it will help to expand agriculture and hence vital food production in the hyper arid region of the Sahara. It is worrying because the source of the water, the Nubian sandstone aquifer system, is considered to be non-renewable and to lie under water-poor regions of Libya, Egypt, Chad and the Sudan. The aquifer may be between 15,000 and 35,000 years old and is a series of connected aquifers extending over 2 million square kilometres, containing approximately 150,000 cubic kilometres of ground water. There are worrying factors built into this project. As the demand for water grows and the aquifer diminishes the technology available to abstract it may become too costly. I suggest that this is what happened to the Garamantes long ago.

Despite his best efforts with these notable projects, the revolutionary zeal which Gaddafi hoped for did not emerge from his new system of People's Congresses. Consequently, he initiated the formation of Revolutionary Committees, ostensibly to mobilise the masses and safeguard the people's rule as exercised through the People's Congresses and People's Committees. The People's Revolutionary Committees were divided into eight regional commandoes reporting directly to Gaddafi through Muhammad Amsaid al Mehjub al Gaddafi. The chief editor of the revolutionary magazine *The Green March* estimated that the Revolutionary Committees had 60,000 members in May 2002.

They were lightly armed and equipped with Jeeps and good telecommunications, and between 1978 and 1980 they were endowed with substantial authority. Their duties included arresting counter-revolutionaries, guaranteeing internal stability, eliminating the enemies of the revolution at home and abroad, and establishing revolutionary courts. These courts were convened by members of the Revolutionary Committees, not by regular judges, and were not bound by an acceptable legal code. In May 1981, Gaddafi outlawed all professions, creating considerable disruption to civil life. In doing so, he abolished the private practice of law. Thus the last vestige of protection a citizen might have expected in the revolutionary courts was removed.

The power of the Revolutionary Committees and their untrammelled revolutionary courts gave undue control over civil life into Gaddafi's hands. The practice of public hangings, televised by the state, was probably only partially reduced with the passing of the Great Green Human Rights Charter in June 1968.

Revolutionary Guards were formed within the armed forces to indoctrinate troops, hold armoury keys and perform other security related tasks. There were a number of refinements to this system, such as the People's Guard, which appeared to specialise in eliminating the Islamist rebels. There were also Purification Committees, which specialised in eliminating nepotism, money fraud, bribery and drug trafficking. In all, the regime exercised very considerable surveillance over the people.

Human Rights Watch

That there have been human rights violations in Libya is now without doubt. There are two incidents that have had direct bearing on the 17 February 2011 uprising in Benghazi.

The Abu Salim families were amongst the first street protesters in Benghazi on 15 February 2011. For some time the Human Rights Watch had been concerned about the alleged massacre at Abu Salim jail in Tripoli. There follows a synopsis of their report of 27 June 2009.

The report is corroborated by the discovery of a mass grave in Tripoli in September 2011. It was based on an interview in the USA with a Libyan asylum seeker called Hussein al Shafa'i, who had been in Abu Salim on political charges from 1988 to 2000. His report suggested that at 4.40 p.m. on 28 June 1996 a number of prisoners had captured a guard and commenced to protest about conditions in the jail. He said that hundreds of prisoners had escaped from their cells to protest and were shot at by guards from the roof. He also said that two top security officials, Abdulla al Senussi and Nasr al Mabruk, arrived to take command. Abdulla had recently been the controller of military intelligence in Libya and the brother-in-law of Gaddafi. He is listed by Interpol as being suspected of subsequent involvement in the massacre of prisoners.

Al Shafa'i stated that Senussi ordered the shooting to stop and called for a delegation to make a case for the prisoners, promising to address their complaints if they returned to their cells and released the two guards they had taken hostage. One guard was released but the other had died.

Al Shafa'i went on to describe what happened the following day:

> At 11.00 on 29th June a hand grenade was thrown into one of the courtyards. I did not see who threw the grenade. I heard the explosion and right after a constant shooting started from heavy weapons and Kalashnikovs from the top of the roof. The shooting continued from 11.00 until 1.35 … I saw the men who did the shooting. They were wearing beige khaki uniforms with green bandanas … Around 2 p.m. the forces used pistols to finish off those who were not dead.

Abu Salim jail held from 1,600 to 1,700 prisoners and al Shafa'i calculated that the security forces shot and killed 1,200. He said that he was able to estimate the number killed because he was a cook. He counted the number of meals prepared in the kitchen before and after the shooting incident.

The Human Rights Watch claims that the al Shafa'i report has been corroborated from a group called the Libyan Human Rights Solidarity, based in Switzerland, who stated that the authorities had notified 112 families that relatives had died in Abu Salim without providing the bodies or giving details of the cause of death. The group also states that 238 families have claimed to have lost contact with a relative who was a prisoner in Abu Salim.

The Libyan International Security Agency denied the accusations. They asserted that more than 400 prisoners escaped Abu Salim jail prior to the incident. Among the escapees, they stated, were men who fought with Islamist militant groups in Afghanistan, Iran and Iraq.[7]

The rise of religiosity in Libya was a problem for Gaddafi, as it has been for many Muslim countries. Gaddafi ruthlessly suppressed it in Libya but sometimes supported it in Algeria and Morocco. He quarrelled with and suppressed the Ulama, that is the religious establishment, many of whom fled the country. Some, such as Sheikh el Bishti a popular imam of Tripoli, are said to have disappeared.

The Muslim Brotherhood, imported into Libya from Egypt, gained a firm foothold in the 1950s. It has since become the Libyan Islamic Group and, at one time, aspired to replace Gaddafi's regime. It was strengthened by Libyan students returning from the USA and the UK who had been radicalised. The group was well supported in and around Benghazi, where opposition to the regime was strongest. Six members of the group were publicly executed in the Benghazi stadium in 1987. The executions were shown on state television.

A more militant group broke away and survived, despite a crackdown. It named itself the Libya Islamic Fighting Group, amongst which were a number of Jihadists who had returned from the conflict in Afghanistan. In 1998 the regime killed some of the group and arrested 103 core members, whom they had held incommunicado in Abu Salim jail for a number of years. Two were eventually executed.[8]

According to the *Tripoli Times* published on 6 February 2010, Dr Huda ben Amer, Secretary of the General People's Council of Inspection People's Control, was sworn in to the Secretariat of the General People's Congress, the Libya Cabinet. She had been twice Mayor of Benghazi and allegations about her have been rife there since the 17 February uprising. She has been referred to as Huda the Executioner for the part she played in a public hanging in the Benghazi baseball stadium. Many in Benghazi suggest that she came to the attention of Gaddafi as a result.

It is said that an aeronautical engineer called al Sadek Hamed al Shuwehdy was executed for alleged dissidence before a large crowd of students and school children who thought they were there to witness a public trial. He was slow to die and whilst he was kicking and writhing on the end of the rope a young woman grasped his legs and pulled him down. People identified the woman as the Gaddafi loyalist Huda ben Amer. It was said that Gaddafi was in the habit of watching public hangings on the television.

Should the allegations made against Huda ben Amer be verified, it would leave little room for the Gaddafi regime to claim that its human rights record was without blemish.

10

Gaddafi III
Weapons of Mass Destruction, the IRA, St James's Square and Lockerbie

Britain has long treated Libya as a rogue state. Gaddafi's efforts to acquire weapons of mass destruction began to alarm observers, especially because he was considered dangerously unpredictable.

The 1984 shooting of a London policewoman from inside the Libyan Embassy, the Libyan arming of the IRA and the 1988 Lockerbie airline bombing over Scotland, for which a Libyan was convicted, contributed to Libya being branded a pariah state.

In 1981 President Ronald Reagan invalidated the use of US passports for travel to Libya and in 1982 the US banned imports of Libyan oil and a number of exports to Libya, following a deterioration of relations. In 1986 a Berlin disco bombing led to sanctions being widened to include a total ban on direct import and export trade, commercial contracts and travel-related activities.

The sanctions brought internal dissent, which eventually forced Gaddafi to seek a rapprochement with the USA and the UK.

Gaddafi and Weapons of Mass Destruction

After Gaddafi closed down the US and British bases in 1970, Libya turned to Egypt for military assistance and to France for the supply of weapons, especially Mirage fighters.

One factor often overlooked by historians of Gaddafi's coup is that soon after it took place Egyptian military units were deployed at strategic points throughout Libya to help prevent a counter-coup. By 1972 around 2,000 Egyptian soldiers were serving in the country as instructors. When the military academy in Benghazi closed, a number of Libyans were trained at the Egyptian military academy. A rift that developed between Gaddafi and President Sadat in 1973 caused Egypt to withdraw its people from Libya. At this time Egypt also withdrew surface-to-air missiles and halted work on the air defences of Tripoli, Benghazi and Tobruk.

Gaddafi had already courted the Soviet Union and in July 1970 the first Soviet military vehicles and equipment arrived in Libya.

After Egypt withdrew, Gaddafi appealed to Pakistan for help and a Pakistani contingent arrived to train Libyan air and ground crews on helicopters and transport aircraft.

The statistics of the Libyan armed forces published by observers vary widely from the few published by the Libyan regime itself. Some authorities have suggested that between 1973 and 1983 Libya spent $28 billion on new armaments. It seems that $20 billion went to the USSR and the Soviet bloc. The military nominal role rose from 7,000 in 1969 to 86,000 in 1988. The number dropped after the war with Chad and again in 2004 to 61,500. Libya was said to have 3,000 tanks, probably the eighth largest such force in the world.

The Libyan army's range of tracked and wheeled armoured vehicles gave it the capacity to deploy readily over long distances. Its rocket systems, engineering equipment, infantry weapons and fire control systems, flame throwers and anti-tank guided missiles were in ample supply.

In 2002, the best assessment suggested that the Libyan army made up about two-thirds of the armed forces at 45,000 men, of which 25,000 were believed to be conscripts.

At the same time the Libyan air force consisted of around 10,000 men and the main air bases were Uqba ibn Nafi, the old USAF base previously called Wheelus, near Tripoli, and Gamal al Nasser at Benina, near Benghazi. The base at Hun, an oasis where Gaddafi's tribe had holdings, was expanded. There were also bases at Kufra, Gebel Unwainat, Sebha and Tobruk. The air defence units were armed with ground-to-air missiles, which were based in five defence regions at the military airfields.

The navy was said to have a nominal role of 6,500 men and its two frigates, three corvettes, numerous speedboats and four submarines were based in Tripoli, Benghazi, Tobruk, Khums, Marsa Brega and Ras Hilal.

However accurate the figures given for Libyan military purchases may be, there can be no doubt that Gaddafi gave priority to the procurement of arms and military materiel over domestic spending. For a long time arms imports represented over half the total defence expenditures.

His problems lay in the sophisticated nature of the armaments and the technology needed to support them. It has been estimated that more than half the equipment he purchased was stored or unserviceable. This was especially so for the Libyan air force, which had been struggling to develop trained air and ground crews to match the acquisition of modern planes and weaponry. It has also been said that Libyan air units were reluctant to commit themselves and did not perform well in air-to-air combat.

The Libyan air force was tested against US navy flyers on at least two occasions over the Gulf of Sirte. In 1973, Gaddafi had claimed much of the gulf to be within Libyan territorial waters. He had drawn a line across it from a point near Benghazi to a headland near Misurata. He called this the Line of Death and said that any hostile power crossing it would be opposed by force of arms. The United States challenged him and conducted naval operations south of the line in August 1981 with the United States Sixth Fleet. Libyan fighter planes were assembled to fly patrols near the American ships. On 19 August, two Libyan Su-22 Fitter fighter-bombers were intercepted by two F-14 Tomcat fighters from the aircraft carrier *Nimitz*. One of the US planes was targeted by an air-to-air Atoll missile. The F-14 evaded the missile and launched Sidewinder 9L missiles in retaliation and both Libyan planes were shot down. The two Libyan pilots managed to eject and were rescued from the sea.

A further clash occurred in 1986 when the US navy sailed a carrier task force across the Line of Death. The Libyan fighters were no match for their US counterparts during a number of engagements.

Foreign governments observing the build-up of military hardware and hearing Gaddafi's belligerent speeches grew increasingly uneasy.[1]

Gaddafi's Islamic Legion, which he formed in 1987, was intended to be the military arm of his policy of expansion. He publicised his plans for it in the Arab press with his usual bravado. It was supposed to consist of 1 million men and women who were to prepare for the great battle to liberate Palestine and overcome imperialism. It never achieved that aspiration, being considerably less in number and noted for its poor morale and military ineptitude.

Unsuspecting recruits for the Islamic Legion came from immigrants seeking work in oil-rich Libya. Amongst them were thousands of Pakistanis who thought they were being recruited for lucrative jobs but found themselves in uniform and sent to fight in Gaddafi's war with Chad. Unfortunately, the 7,000 legionaries he sent there were routed ignominiously.

Gaddafi also maintained a force of 2,000 Islamic legionaries in the Darfur province in the Sudan. He disbanded the legion in 1987, but a number remained in Darfur to form a hard core of the Janjaweed, the racist army of Arab supremacists that has caused so much misery.[2]

Greater unease was created in some quarters by the reports about Gaddafi's efforts to acquire weapons of mass destruction and missiles capable of reaching targets in Israel and Europe.

Some observers discounted Libya's nuclear capabilities because of its failure to procure important components and a lack of engineering and scientific skills. We now know that Gaddafi was being supplied the equipment with the help of Dr Abdul Qadeer Khan, the scientist then in charge of Pakistan's nuclear enrichment facility. To make nuclear-grade uranium from the raw material it needs to be passed through a cascade of centrifuges in a process referred to as enrichment. The centrifuges are difficult to manufacture and harder to obtain because of international laws prohibiting their sale. There were companies that made them and sold them on the black market, one of which was in Malaya. Through Khan, the Libyans acquired a number of these centrifuges from this company and ordered many more. The Libyans managed to erect three cascades, but only one that worked.

Khan also supplied Gaddafi's scientists with the plans to make a nuclear bomb, which they were unable to understand. They were incomplete in any case. One source thought that the plans were similar to those used by China in the 1960s. Khan's bomb, were it to be constructed, would not have fitted the North Korean SCUD-C short-range ballistic missile, of which the Libyans possessed at least five. They were trying to purchase North Korean No Dong missiles, with a range of 1,400km, happily without success.

Between 1980 and 1990, Libya had also prepared 23 tons of mustard gas in the facility at Rabta and had thousands of unfilled chemical munitions in storage.

In March 2004, the USA removed over 1,000 tons of centrifuge and missile parts from Libya as part of the disarmament process when Gaddafi agreed to give up weapons of mass destruction. Russia also removed 13kg of fresh 80 per cent highly enriched uranium from the 10-megawat research centre at Tajura. However, at least two accounts suggest that Gaddafi had offered to renounce his weapons of mass destruction programme in 1992 and again in 1999, perhaps because it was not working.[3]

Gaddafi and the IRA

The Irish Republican Army's link with Gaddafi lasted more than thirty years. It allowed the IRA to prolong its terror campaign and had a direct effect on the number of deaths and casualties. Probably every bomb constructed by the Provisional IRA and its splinter groups has contained Semtex from a Libyan shipment unloaded at an Irish pier in 1986. Victims of the IRA bombing campaign are seeking compensation from Libya.[4]

There is no doubt that Gaddafi intended use the IRA connection to hurt the UK as much as he could, especially after it allowed the Americans to use Upper Heyford in Oxfordshire as a base for the American F-111s that bombed Tripoli in April 1986, killing his stepdaughter, Hannah, and a number of Libyans.

Gaddafi had a naive view of the Northern Ireland problem. Paul Loughlin, a producer on RTÉ's *Today Tonight* was filming Gaddafi in Tripoli in October 1986. Loughlin had a conversation with him during the filming and later wrote:

I asked Gadafy [sic] whether he was aware that there were one million Protestants in Northern Ireland who opposed the aims of the IRA and who lived in fear of them. Gadafy asked how many Catholics there were in the island of Ireland and how many Protestants. I replied that the figures rounded out to something more than four million Catholics and over a million Protestants. Gadafy said that meant the Catholics were in the right. Clearly in his mind if you were a Catholic you should be in the IRA and if you were a Protestant you were a colonist.

Gaddafi's support for the IRA started in 1972 when the notable republican, Joe Cahill, was invited to go to Tripoli to arrange for arms shipments and financial aid. Gaddafi had been impressed by his courage and there is no doubt that Cahill was a sincere believer in his cause.

Cahill met Gaddafi at Bab Azzizia and gave him a shopping list of weaponry he wanted for his war on the British forces in Northern Ireland. At the time the IRA was reliant on the USA for arms and finance, principally through NORIAD, an organisation with connections in high places and considerable influence. The CIA was making some progress in finding and stopping arms shipments and the IRA wanted new sources.

In March 1973, the first shipment of arms from Libya was put aboard the *Claudia*, a boat registered in Cyprus. The arrangements made to charter the *Claudia* were to be Joe Cahill's Achilles' heel. They were made by a German who may have been less than discreet. The *Claudia* had a history of smuggling operations and the Libyans were wary of it, with good reason.

The *Claudia* was supposed to rendezvous in international waters off Tripoli, where a cargo of about 50 tons of arms was to be transhipped. In the event, the *Claudia*'s radio was unserviceable. Her crew could not communicate with the Libyans to give her position as arranged, so, against orders, she entered harbour to the consternation of Cahill and his helpers. The British had closed their embassy in Tripoli following the shooting of PC Fletcher, but both the Libyans and the IRA were wary of spies observing events around the docks, probably with good reason. Nevertheless, they loaded part of the promised cargo of arms and the *Claudia* made for Ireland with Cahill aboard.

There are some reports that the *Claudia* appears to have been spotted and probably shadowed by a submarine.[5] There is no doubt that it was betrayed to the Irish government in some way. However, it reached Irish waters off Waterford. It was about to offload its cargo when the Irish naval service appeared and boarded it, capturing Joe Cahill and a number of his associates. He was sentenced to jail for three years on 21 May 1973.

How the *Claudia* operation was betrayed is still not clear. Blundy and Lycett came to the conclusion that Gaddafi himself gave too much information away and alerted the intelligence services.[6]

A family friend with business links with Libya was in the UK at about the time of the incident and was visited by a British diplomat he had previously met in Libya, who wanted information on arms shipments. He was unable to help.

Between August 1985 and September 1986, four significant arms shipment from Libya were landed without detection in the Republic of Ireland. The first was shipped in the *Casamara*, a British-registered 65ft yacht owned and skippered by Adrian Hopkins, an unsuccessful travel agent. It rendezvoused with a Libyan ship, the *Samra Africa*, off the Maltese island of Gozo and loaded 10 tons of arms and ammunition, including AK-47 rifles, Brazilian-manufactured hand guns and Bulgarian RPG rockets. It set sail for Ireland in August 1985.

The *Casamara*, renamed the *Kula*, returned for a second cargo in October 1985, again picking up 10 tons of arms off Gozo and landing them in Ireland at Clogga Strand, near Arkland. The shipment contained some powerful Second World War Russian 'Dushkas', heavy machine guns intended to bring down British army helicopters in South Armagh.

The *Kula* made a further trip in April 1986, which yielded between 15 and 20 tons of arms and ammunition, including SAM ground-to-air missiles, also intended to bring down British army helicopters. The missiles proved useless to the IRA as they were too complicated. This was the shipment, however, that contained the 6 tons of Semtex which proved to be the deadliest weapon in IRA hands. It revolutionised the IRA campaign. Their bombers became skilled in the construction of Improvised Explosive Devices (IEDs), which they were to use

both in Northern Ireland and in Britain. They were the fore-
runners of those used in Afghanistan to kill and maim so many.

The biggest shipment to get through came in September
1986. For this a larger ship, the *Villa*, was used. The cargo
seems to have amounted to 80 or 90 tones of weaponry,
including three SAM missiles, more than 1,000 AK-47s and
more Semtex. By now the IRA was nearly as well armed as
the security forces and its hard liners were contemplating an
open, all-out offensive against British troops. The long efforts
by Gerry Adams to convert the armed struggle into a political
one were severely undermined by the huge quantity of arms
from Libya. When the USA came under direct terrorist attack
on 11 September it became clear that the IRA would not be
able to use its SAMs and Semtex with the same freedom.

The last shipment was to be detected and intercepted by the
French off Brest in October 1987. It was aboard the *Eksund*,
a small cargo vessel, and was carrying 150 tons of weapons,
including twenty SAM missiles and 1,000 mortars. There
is evidence that the shipment was betrayed from inside the
IRA. From the time it left Libya, it was being monitored by
the British and French intelligence services and tracked by
a Royal Navy hunter-killer submarine. The capture of the
Eksund was greeted with a brief period of euphoria by the
British intelligence community until the interrogation of one
of the crew revealed the previous four shipments and they
realised that they had failed to detect them.[7]

Gaddafi and the Murder of PC Yvonne Fletcher

Gaddafi focused much of his personal attention on defectors
and students living in exile in the US, Britain, Egypt, Morocco
and the Sudan. There and elsewhere, some of them had formed
opposition movements, amongst which were the National
Front for the Salvation of Libya, the Libyan Constitutional
Union, the Libyan Democratic National Rally and the Islamic
Association of Libya.

Gaddafi had attempted to disrupt and intimidate them and,
between 1980 and 1984, had been responsible for the murder

of some fifteen exiles. He was afraid that these groups might mount a coup against him.

He was particularly interested in Britain, where there were around 8,000 Libyan students. He was sure they were being subverted by dissident groups. He was also sure that these groups were backed by MI5 and the CIA. Therefore, he decided to form loyalist Revolutionary Committees amongst Libyan students studying in Britain. They were to try to neutralise the largest opposition group, the National Front for the Salvation of Libya, which had a considerable student following.

The Libyan Embassy in London, which was known as the Libyan People's Bureau, had been taken over by a Revolutionary Committee made up of students loyal to Gaddafi, a prominent member of which was Dr Omar Sodani, who was studying at the Royal School of Tropical Medicine.

Sodani was typical of the hard core Gaddafi loyalists. He was born to a poor and illiterate family in the Fezzan, where he attended primary school. He was picked to go to one of the Revolutionary Committee schools. There were a handful of these selective schools in Gaddafi's Libya, one of which was the famous Reactionary Blooms School in Benghazi. They specialised in the intensive indoctrination of adolescents with the revolutionary thoughts and principles of Gaddafi's *Green Book*.

Sodani was an apt pupil and entered the Gar Yunis University in Benghazi to study medicine. He was president of the Students' Union and a key member of the student Revolutionary Committee. Blundy and Lycett suggest that he presided over the execution of two counter-revolutionaries, thus earning the not exclusive nickname of 'the Butcher of Benghazi'.[8]

Gaddafi had ordered his Revolutionary Committee to eliminate his enemies, whom he dubbed stray dogs. In March 1984, eight bombs exploded at anti-Gaddafi targets in Manchester and London. Relations between the Revolutionary Committees and the National Front had become heated and made Gaddafi nervous. He insisted that his loyalists in London should precipitate some action, which would ultimately result in the expulsion of the National Front from Britain.[9]

Omar Sodani called a meeting of Revolutionary Committees in London and made it clear that they were to take action against the anti–Gaddafi National Front. Emissaries were sent to the pro–Gaddafi Students Revolutionary Committees around the country to stir them up in anticipation of a forthcoming event of significance.

It is likely that, on 16 April 1984, a telex from Gaddafi instructing his embassy in London to use violence against the National Front was intercepted by GCHQ in Cheltenham, but it lay on a desk and was not decoded for some time.[10]

On 17 April 1984, about seventy-five protesters from the National Front for the Salvation of Libya arrived outside the embassy in St James's Square by coach and commenced a demonstration.

A counter-demonstration, organised by the Libyan Embassy, was also in the square. The two groups were kept apart by crowd-control barriers and Metropolitan police officers. In the middle of the police ranks was PC Yvonne Fletcher.

The demonstration began peacefully, with the crowd kept apart by the barriers. Both groups shouted at each other and waved banners and placards. At some time, Omar Sodani appears to have left the Libyan Embassy and entered the square to remonstrate with the contractor who had erected the barriers. He was arrested by the police for causing an altercation. It seems he had wanted the barriers removed so that it would be possible for the pro-Gaddafi group to capture some National Front demonstrators and drag them into the embassy. The barriers were not removed and the demonstration continued, with both sides exchanging insults and slogans.

At 10.20 a.m. a burst of shots was fired from a first-floor window of the embassy and a number of National Front protesters were hit. PC Yvonne Fletcher fell to the ground, wounded by a single shot. Her fiancé, also policing the demonstration, was able to comfort her. She died later in hospital. The image on national television of police helmets lying abandoned in the little square of St James's was to turn British public opinion against the Gaddafi regime.

The pro-Gaddafi demonstrators vanished, and the police surrounded the embassy and laid siege to it for eleven days as they were prevented by the COBRA committee of the government from entering it. The government may have been cautious because there were 8,000 or so Britons living in

Libya and Gaddafi was known to take revenge on expatriates of countries that upset him.

Gaddafi accused the British of attacking his Libyan People's Bureau and sent soldiers to lay siege to the British Embassy in Tripoli.

Protracted negotiations ensued, which resulted in the occupants of both embassies claiming diplomatic immunity and leaving under guard. The Libyan diplomats were flown home. They were never interrogated by the British police and they may have removed the murder weapon in a diplomatic bag.

After they left, their embassy was searched and Omar Sodani's fingerprints were found on the ledge of the first-floor window presumed to have been where the shots had been fired. No one was charged with Yvonne Fletcher's murder.

Diplomatic relations between Libya and Britain were broken off and were not restored until 1999. However, officers from the Metropolitan Police visited Libya and interviewed witnesses. They were relatively confident that they knew two possible suspects.

There is some controversy surrounding the ballistic evidence submitted to the Crown. Tam Dalyell MP has drawn attention to the following: 'George Stiles, the senior ballistics officer of the British Army, who said that, as a ballistics expert, he believed that the WPC could not have been killed from the first floor of the Libyan Embassy, as was suggested.'[11]

The conspiracy theories surrounding the shooting of Yvonne Fletcher are still alive, despite the admission of general responsibility by the Gaddafi regime.

In March 2011, the authorities in Benghazi captured Omar Sodani, the head of the al Ejanalghoria, Muammar Gaddafi's militia in Benghazi, and placed him under arrest. He was later interviewed by news reporters outside the Benghazi jail. He was questioned about the shooting of PC Yvonne Fletcher and was asked about the allegations that he provided reports on Libyan students in London, which had led to their persecution.

Mr Sodani pointed out that he was in police custody when the shooting of PC Fletcher took place, as the evidence shows. He may, however, be able to shed some light on the events in St James's Square on that fateful day.[12]

The Lockerbie Killings

Just after 7 p.m. on Wednesday 21 December 1988, Pan American World Airways flight 103 exploded over Lockerbie in Scotland, killing 259 passengers and crew and 11 people on the ground. There is a great deal of information in the public domain about this event and its aftermath, and the victims and relatives must hope that much of the speculation it has generated is soon resolved. Unfortunately, no account of the trial of those accused of perpetrating the crime can be free of controversy.

British and US air accident investigators concluded that the Pan American Boeing 747-121 had been destroyed by a Semtex bomb enclosed in a Toshiba Bombeat cassette recorder packed in a brown Samsonite-type suitcase, which had been loaded in a container in the forward hold.

They also concluded that the bomb had been detonated by a MST-13 timing device. Twenty such devices were said to have been sold by the Swiss company MEBO to a Libyan. In the remains of the suitcase the investigators found remnants of clothing purchased in a shop in Malta.

Two Libyans were accused of murder and conspiracy to murder, and of breaching the Aviation Security Act of 1982. They were Abdelbaset Ali Mohammad al Megrahi and al Amin Khalifa Fhimah. They were both identified as Libyan Arab Airline officials. Al Megrahi was said to have been the airline's security manager and Fhimah its sometime station manager in Malta. A witness, Abdul Majid Giaka, also a sometime official of Libyan Arab Airlines working in Malta, testified that Megrahi was an agent of the Libyan External Security Agency, known as the ESO. Giaka was a CIA asset who had been employed by the Libyan ESO in a minor capacity. His evidence has been the subject of much criticism and was deemed unreliable except in that it identified Megrahi as a member of the ESO.

Clothing that the crash investigators identified as being in the suitcase bomb was traced to a shop called Mary's House in Sliema, Malta. The shop belonged to Tony Gauci. He was questioned and identified Megrahi as the customer who had entered the shop and purchased the clothing, probably on 7 December 1988. Gauci's evidence has been challenged, but Megrahi was in Malta at the time.

The proprietors of the Swiss firm MEBO identified Megrahi as having been involved in the procurement of the MST-13 timer device found in the vicinity of the crash in Scotland. Their evidence was not always impressive. There is a great deal of circumstantial evidence that Megrahi was involved, which may come to light when and if the Libyan files are opened for review. It has also been stated that the particular MST-13 devices were sold only to Libya.

There is some uncertainty surrounding this part of the evidence and it is summed up in the following extract from a speech by the MP for Linlithgow, Tam Dalyell, in parliament in 1997:

> The Crown Office must consider many other aspects of the legal case. It must forgive our curiosity about how much can be built up from the so-called 'forensic evidence' of a slither of micro-circuitry found we do not know when, by whom or in what circumstances, but subject, it appears, to a Scottish winter.

The evidence taken together led to Megrahi and Fhimah being accused of placing a radio cassette player containing Semtex and a timing device into a suitcase and somehow arranging for it to be forwarded as unaccompanied baggage, first from Luqa by Malta Airways flight KM180 to Frankfurt and then on the Pan Am feeder flight 103A to Heathrow, where it was loaded into the forward cargo hold of Pan American Airways flight PA103.

Documentary evidence obtained from the Frankfurt baggage-handling organisation is important because it shows that an item of luggage was transferred from the Malta Airways flight to the Pan American feeder flight. In order for this to happen the bag must have been properly tagged. The tag would have ensured that the standard interline baggage procedure was followed to transfer it from one airline to another and forward it to its destination, in this case JFK Airport, New York. The process is used to reunite passengers with baggage lost by the airlines. I have initiated this procedure myself on behalf of passengers of East African Airways. My experience leads me to comment that there were a number of possible delays and errors built into the process and I am surprised it was chosen as a method of planting a bomb on PA103.

The tags used for the procedure are usually kept locked up and are issued to staff with care. Malta Airways strenuously defend the security procedure surrounding the issue of these labels. However, the British and Americans argued that Fhimah illegally obtained some labels for Megrahi, though this was never proved in court.

The prosecution case was that Megrahi used an alias to travel from Tripoli to Malta, together with Fhimah, on the evening of 20 December 1988. He was said to be travelling as Ahmed Khalifa Abdusamad on a passport issued by the Libyan passport authority. It was supposed that Fhimah, as the former station manager of Libyan Arab Airlines at Luqa airport, would be familiar with the Air Malta staff and the procedures used there for shipping unaccompanied baggage.

It was asserted that Megrahi and Fhimah brought a large, brown Samsonite suitcase with them into Malta on that occasion.

The Malta Airways records show that, on 21 December, baggage for KM180 was being handled at about the same time as that of Libyan Arab Airlines flight LN147 from Luqa to Tripoli. It was suggested that there was an opportunity for someone familiar with the processes to have inserted the bag into the system at this time. Al Megrahi, travelling as Abdusamad, boarded the LN147 bound for Tripoli on the morning of 21 December 1988 at Luqa airport.

However, the suggestion that the bag could have been inserted into the system should be treated with care and considered alongside the following extract from a statement made by the MP for Linlithgow, Tam Dalyell, in the British parliament and reported in the *Guardian* on Wednesday 23 July 1997: 'The hard fact is that, in a court case, Air Malta won damages against Grenada Television for suggesting that it was lax or involved. The Maltese Government, the Maltese police, the airport authorities and Air Malta do not accept that unidentified baggage left Valetta airport.'

The USA and the UK attempted to extradite Megrahi and Fhimah for trial, but the Libyan government refused.

In April 1992 the UN Security Council imposed an air and arms embargo and banned the sale of oil equipment to Libya to put pressure on Tripoli to comply.

A great deal of international effort was expended in attempting to persuade Gaddafi to give up the suspects for trial in the US or UK. In the end he agreed to send them for trial under Scottish law before judges but not a jury. He insisted that the trial should be on neutral ground. Sanctions were suspended in April 1999 when they were surrendered for trail.

The trial of the two men accused of placing a bomb on Pan Am flight 103 opened in the Netherlands on 3 May 2000, at a specially convened Scottish court set up under Scots law and held at a disused United States Air Force base called Camp Zeist, near Utrecht.

The Scottish judges were men of impeccable reputation and long experience. They were Lord Sutherland, Lord Coulsfield and Lord MacLean, who were assisted by Lord Abernethy. Despite this, controversy still surrounds the trial and its aftermath.

In view of this, the judgement of the court is important. It states in part:

> ... we are satisfied that it has been proved that the primary suitcase containing the explosive device was dispatched from Malta, passed through Frankfurt and was loaded onto PA103 at Heathrow. It is clear that with one exception the clothing in the primary suitcase was the clothing purchased in Mr Gauci's shop, Mary's House at Sliema, on 7 December 1988. The purchaser was, on Mr Gauci's evidence, a Libyan.
>
> The trigger for the explosion was an MST-13 timer of the single solder mask variety. A substantial quantity of such timers had been supplied to Libya ... When, however, the evidence regarding the clothing, the purchaser and the timer is taken with the evidence that an unaccompanied bag was taken from KM180 to PA103A, the inference that that it was the primary suitcase becomes, in our view, irresistible ... we remain of the view that the primary suitcase began its journey at Luqa.

As to Megrahi, the judgement states:

> It is possible to infer that this visit under a false name the
> night before the explosive device was planted at Luqa, fol-
> lowed by his departure for Tripoli the following morning at
> or about the time the device must have been planted, was a
> visit connected with the planting of the device.

The court convicted Abdelbaset al Megrahi of murder on
31 January 2001. The second accused, al Amin Khalifa Fhimah,
was acquitted. The complete ruling is available from the
Scottish courts.

It is interesting to compare the story of Pan Am 103 with
the later case of Union des Transports Aériens flight number
772, which was blown up in 1989. This has been called the
forgotten flight. On 19 September 1989 a DC10 of the French
airline UTA, flight number 772, was flying from N'Djamena
International Airport in Congo Brazzaville to Paris. It
exploded over the Sahara Desert in southern Niger, killing
170 people. The wreckage was sent to France where air accident investigators found traces of an explosive called pentrite
in the forward hold. Pentrite is mixed with other compounds
to form Semtex. A dark grey Samsonite suitcase was found
covered with a layer of pentrite. The suitcase had been loaded
at Brazzaville. Part of a timing devise was found. It was traced
back to Libya.[13] A court in Paris tried and convicted six
Libyans in absentia of causing the explosion.

On 15 August 2003, Libya formally accepted responsibility
for the actions of its officials with regard to the Lockerbie disas-
ter and agreed to pay $2.7 billion in compensation to relatives of
those killed in the attack. Britain then drafted a Security Council
resolution to end UN sanctions. A further Libyan agreement to
compensate for the 1989 bombing of the French UTA airliner
led to the resolution being passed on 12 September 2003.

On 20 September 2004, President George W. Bush lifted
the American trade embargo on Libya. Most of the sanctions
were suspended in April 2004, but the president formally
revoked those which remained – dealing with general trade,
aviation and importing Libyan oil. A freeze on Libyan assets in
the US was also lifted.

Britain had restored diplomatic relations with Libya in 1999 after Libya had accepted general responsibility for the murder of PC Yvonne Fletcher.

Megrahi had appealed against his conviction. It was rejected on 24 March 2002. However, in 2007 the Scottish Criminal Cases Review Commission granted him a second appeal. His second appeal got under way in 2009, but shortly afterwards applications were made for both his transfer to a Libyan jail and release on compassionate grounds.

As he was in the advanced stage of prostate cancer, on 20 August 2009, the Scottish justice minister, Kenny McAskill, released him to die in Libya. His arrival in Tripoli was greeted with acclaim and the relationship between the US and the UK was severely tested. The Americans were not in favour of his release. His second appeal was dropped. This has caused some frustration amongst those who disagreed with the original conviction.

The Burden of Power in Libya

By handing over the Lockerbie suspects for trial, Gaddafi had opened the way to the ending of the crippling sanctions imposed on Libya by the USA. His people had suffered enough. His education policy had produced numerous young people ready for work but there were no jobs for them.

Lying beneath the deserts and the Gulf of Sirte was a potential reserve of oil and natural gas. To get at it he needed American experts and equipment. The existing oil fields were served by outdated technology and isolation had crushed enterprise and innovation. Some of the brightest and best Libyans were living in exile and opposition to his rule was mounting. He could not continue to kill his enemies at home or overseas. His human rights record was appalling and we have yet to learn the full extent of his killings. His sons were eager for his crown and he was beginning to watch his back. He had to come to terms with the USA and he used the British as brokers.

There is no better illustration of this than the event on 29 May 2007, when the British prime minister Tony Blair met Muammar Gaddafi in a Bedouin tent in the Libyan Desert south of the city of Sirte. The meeting was to demonstrate to the world that there was a rapprochement between Gaddafi and the British.

For Blair it was a stop on a tour of Africa designed to impress his home audience with the successes he had achieved with his interventionist foreign policy. For Gaddafi, this was a public relations coup of considerable significance. He needed to sell his sudden turnaround to the Libyan people. He had told them often enough that the British were the arch-enemy, now he was coming to terms with them.

The tent was pitched in the land of his tribe, the Gaddadfa, where he went to primary school at the age of 10. It was not lost on many observers that the nearby shores of the Gulf of Sirte are where much of the oil from the desert was shipped to provide the wealth to keep him in power. Following Blair's visit, BP announced that they would be drilling for oil in the Gulf of Sirte.

In hindsight, Prime Minister Blair may have seen it as a moment when pragmatism had blinded him to prudence. Later he was to argue that Gaddafi had renounced his nuclear ambitions and had told MI6 where the centrifuge technology came from – the so-called nuclear bazaar in Pakistan.

The intelligence coup that enriched the CIA and MI6 was, perhaps, worth a moment of humility in the desert. In addition, Tony Blair claimed that the flow of economic migrants and asylum seekers into Europe would be stemmed by a more diligent Libya, whose coastline had been leaking them into Italy at an alarming rate.

Gaddafi's efforts to bring Libya in from the cold were too late. Young, well-educated Libyans had begun to see his posturing as both lethal and comic, and open ridicule destroys dictators quickly.

The people of Benghazi had never been docile. The hangings in the baseball stadium and the oppressive rule of people like Huda ben Amer and Omar Sodani had pushed them beyond fear. They were angry enough to die for freedom. They began to do so on 17 February 2011.

11

Challenging Muammar Gaddafi

For more than forty years Colonel Muammar Gaddafi dominated Libya. His inhumane treatment of prisoners in one of his jails was to play a major part in his fall from power.

The uprising of 17 February 2011 against the Gaddafi regime in Benghazi, and its aftermath in Libya, has still to be thoroughly and authoritatively analysed outside diplomatic and intelligence circles. However, its place in the history of modern Libya is pivotal.

Since 17 February 2011, Libya has passed a point of no return, but whatever the humanitarian, religious or political issues that will need attention in the future, the key questions will still be who gets the oil and what will they do with it. The simple fact that Libya's oil wealth was not used to establish an equitable society and a democratic government will test the resolve and competence of its future leaders.

The history of Libya is, therefore, interesting because it shows us that its people long languished under foreign occupation before it gained independence and then under two governments, which were more concerned for their own preservation than for the development of a functioning democracy.

It will be the events that took place in Benghazi between 17 and 20 February 2011 which will long be significant in Libya's history. It may all become clearer with time, but it seems that it started as a small street demonstration on 15 February, superficially similar to those in Tunis and Cairo.

There were a number of reasons for discontent in Benghazi. One group, however, claims to have lit the fuse that created the explosion. We might call them the 'Abu Salim Families', for they consist, in the main, of the relatives of those who were massacred in the Abu Salim jail in Tripoli in June 1996. Lindsey Hilsum met some of them on Tuesday 1 March 2011 in Benghazi and filed a report for British Channel 4 News. In the flurry of events, this important report has been largely forgotten, but it should not have been.

She spoke to a number of mothers whose sons were prisoners in the Abu Salim jail and had disappeared without trace for many years. They had been detained without trial and the lawyer for the group in Benghazi, Fathi Turbil, appears to have made frequent representations to the authorities to have them found and tried in open court. He was arrested, some say not for the first time, on 15 February 2011. The 'Families' took to the streets in protest.

The 'Abu Salim Families' formed the nucleus of the protesters, which many thought were copycat Arab Spring demonstrations similar to the Tunisian and Egyptian street revolutions. The Abu Salim massacre had made the Benghazi protest different. Fathi Turbil told Lindsey Hilsum: 'We, the Abu Salim families, ignited the revolution ... The Libyan people were ready to rise up because of the injustice they experienced in their lives but they needed a cause. So calling for the release of people, including me, who had been arrested, became the justification for their protest.' The Human Rights Watch has produced a paper about this dreadful crime in which numerous prisoners were said to have been slaughtered.

In Benghazi's streets, however, matters seemed to have gone from bad to worse when a crowd attempted to attack the army barracks. This was the true seat of Gaddafi's power and word has it that its commandant was one of his sons, al Saadi Gaddafi, well known on the international playboy circuit. There were enough of Gaddafi's kinsmen in the barracks to bolster al Saadi's authority.

At first the rebel attack was inconclusive, but soon the army began to shoot to kill. Rumour has it that al Saadi himself gave the order to shoot, but this needs further corroboration. The killing was awful, but the gates of the barracks were breached on 20 February by a suicide bomber in an explosive-filled automobile. The name of this young man was Almahdi Ziou and it will, no doubt, be long remembered. It was a martyr's death. The breach was stormed by the braver rebels and the depot was surrendered. They were, it seems, armed only with courage and petrol bombs.

After this, the secret police vanished from their lair and left it to be trashed and burnt. This was the place where files were compiled on Gaddafi's enemies, his potential enemies and those against whom the police bore a grudge – echoes of the East German Stasi.

Al Saadi and his henchmen fled to Tripoli, as did Huda ben Amer, sometime mayor of Benghazi. She was later seen on television alongside her mentor, Gaddafi, as he ranted at the crowd from the walls of Tripoli castle. Were she to return to Benghazi, nasty things would certainly occur.

Somehow a rebel army coalesced, found some arms, some transport and an abundance of rhetoric, with which they rushed off to take Tripoli and liberate Libya.

The brief summary which follows hardly does justice to the historic but quixotic attack by a ragtag rebel army along the coast road from Benghazi to Wadi ben Jawad in the Sirtica.

The rebels, with Gaddafi's army apparently fleeing before them, rushed off down the road to take the key town of Ajadabia, the old Senussi capital. By 4 March they were attacking Ras Lanuf, a military barracks and navy dockyard. On 6 March the rebels, by now seriously believing they were on their way to the aid of their friends in Tripoli, were stopped at Wadi ben Jawad by superior forces.

Whilst the twenty-two-nation Arab League readily agreed to support the rebels, they had been forced out of Ras Lanuf again and were trailing back to the oil port of Marsa Brega. Gaddafi's forces soon drove them back to Ajadabia, which they claimed to have recaptured on 15 March, and were in retreat towards Benghazi.

The rebel centres in Cyrenaica were now subjected to air and artillery attack, whilst Saif al Islam, Gaddafi's son, made a remarkable television broadcast from Tripoli, stating that the war would be over in forty-eight hours and advising rebels to take advantage of an amnesty to surrender – advice which they rejected.

On 17 March, the UN Security Council voted to authorise military intervention (the establishment of a No Fly Zone) whilst fighting continued. On 19 March, coalition missiles, largely American but some British, hit Gaddafi's command and control centres, whilst rebels came under severe attack.

By 20 March, the rebels, now in Benghazi again, were facing a ferocious attack and the city was under siege. The possibility of heavy air raids was looming. By 27 March the coalition attacks on Gaddafi's command and control, communications, tanks and aircraft tipped the balance in favour of the rebels, who retook the strategic town of Ajadabia.

Benghazi is a city that Gaddafi hated. His rule there was certainly ruthless and many people had disappeared into his police cells forever. It is not without irony that Benghazi was where Gaddafi's coup took place on 1 September 1969. He cannot have been all that happy about Derna, Baida and Tobruk, towns further to the east, for they fell quickly to the rebels. Throughout their history they had been isolated by distance and the desert, and developed a character of their own. In these towns and their hinterlands had flourished the tribal powerhouse of the Amir of Cyrenaica, who became the King of Libya. Significantly, it was the flag of the old Kingdom of Libya that the rebels brandished so bravely against the green banner of the pro-Gaddafi forces.

What were the 17 February rebels up against? This is how Gaddafi's military might stacked up: there were 50,000 ground forces, give or take a few. His air force personnel strength was around 18,000 and his navy stood at near 8,000. He had 2,205 tanks, 227 jet fighters, 35 attack helicopters and 2 submarines.[1]

The rebels were credited by *The Times* on 6 March with a force of 20,000 armed with AK-47 rifles, mortar bombs, anti-aircraft guns, tanks and pick-up trucks mounted with heavy machine guns. The Libyan regular army units based at Derna, Tobruk and Baida abandoned their bases in the early days of the uprising, allowing the rebels access to their arms and ammunition. General Suleiman Mohammed, the head of the 8th Army based in Tobruk, was one of the important senior officers to join the rebels. Even so, the military balance was heavily in favour of Gaddafi and the rebel forces had yet to develop a unified leadership and strategy.

To take up the story of the seesaw battle for East Libya again: Gaddafi, threatened by the NATO No Fly Zone, which targeted both his heavy armour, his air force and his command and control centres, made a rapid withdrawal from Benghazi and distributed arms amongst the civilian population as he did so. By 26 March the rebels had retaken Ajadabia and by the 29th had reached Sirte, but had been thrown back by Gaddafi's counter-offensive. By 10 April the rebels were back in Ajadabia and a stalemate looked likely. A US military assessment on 22 April confirmed a stalemate existed. The old province of Cyrenaica, east of Ajadabia, was in rebel hands.[2]

How did Gaddafi play his hand? He needed time to find out what support he could muster, settle the confusion amongst his military commanders, ship in mercenaries, tap into his secret funds and organise his logistics. He appears, from news reports, to have brought in mercenaries from Chad, Niger and Mali on 14 February. If this is true, it suggests that he anticipated an uprising. He needed to call in some debts from his friends further afield in Africa, South America and Belarus.

His army was of uncertain loyalty. His air force was loyal, but two Mirage fighter jets had been flown to Malta by defecting pilots. His secret services were likely to be shaky and his enemies were waiting for an opportunity to take him down. He had antagonised a number of tribes, notably the Warfella, and had to cover his back against them.

His publicity machine highlighted the presence of the militant jihadists, of which there are a good number in Cyrenaica, and raised the possibility that they would take control of the anti-Gaddafi military response and create a Somalia in the Mediterranean. That they may still do so is one of the nightmares facing the West and the interim leadership in Libya.

Gaddafi may have hoped that the effect of this on non-interventionist politicians and public opinion in the West would restrain the belligerence of NATO members and promote discord in the Arab League. He may also have calculated that the British and US, war weary and mired as they are in Afghanistan, would be paralysed by public disquiet over the role of militant Islamists in Libya.

The likelihood of a militant jihadist takeover in Libya would have been less than welcome in neighbouring Egypt, where the situation was still potentially volatile. Algeria and Tunisia would have been uneasy since both had been experiencing a rise in religiosity.

The tactical considerations may have taken the following shape in the event of a rebel breakout from Benghazi. Gaddafi would have expected the 17 February rebels to follow his withdrawal to Ajadabia, the importance of which is clear enough from the map, as it controls the roads from Tripolitania to Benghazi and Tobruk. This would stretch the rebels out along an open road and attenuate their logistical support. He could absorb the attacks and commence to degrade their forces with his superior armour and hope that they would expend their ammunition, lives, gasoline and water.

If they took Ajadabia he knew they would rush to capture Marsa Brega and the other oil ports in the Sirtica and fetch up against his base at Ras Lanuf, thus stretching their supply lines even further. The control of the oil ports and the water supply was, and remains, a key focus. It is believed that pressure was brought on Gaddafi to cut the 'Great Man Made River' pipeline carrying water to Benghazi, but that has not occurred.

A further tactical card in his hand was the presence of numerous foreign technicians in the oil fields, the evacuation of whom would be necessary before the West could respond militarily. This would buy him time with which to degrade the 17 February rebel forces.

The wider considerations as the conflict developed are interesting. Gaddafi's diplomatic efforts, if we may call them that, had bought or subverted the governments of the community of the Sahel-Saharan states (Burkina-Faso, Chad, Niger, Mali and the Sudan) so that his southern borders were secure. He had also subverted a number of other doubtful African governments from whom he might expect tacit support or neutrality at least. His recent presidency of the African Union was not without consequence.

His threat to cut off oil exports and his heavy overseas investments would have made some governments hesitate about interfering against him. Some examples will make the point. *The Times* of London reported that 1.49 million barrels of oil were loaded for export by all the Libyan oil terminals in January 2011, of which 85 per cent went to Europe. The *New York Times* reported on 22 February 2011 that the natural gas Greenstream pipeline from Libya to Sicily, which supplied 10 per cent of Italy's consumption, had been closed down. This is a double-edged sword, of course, because Libya is likely to need Greenstream and so there is a mutual interest in keeping it open. However, the shutdown contributed to uncertainty in both Italy and Greece. The UK's visible exports to Libya stood at £423 million in 2009 and are likely to have been higher at the start of the rebellion, as will the £244 million invisible exports recorded in 2008.[3]

The rebellion in West Libya has been harder to follow because of heavy-handed news management by the Gaddafi regime. However, three other centres of rebellion emerged. Probably the most important was in Misurata. This quickly erupted into violence. There are two points to make.

Firstly, Misurata is situated on the coast road from Tripoli to the east. From Misurata the road turns south to skirt the Gulf of Sirte. It threatens vital supply lines and was thus important to both sides. Secondly, Misuratans have been inclined to act independently for many years and have close ties with Benghazi. The propaganda war had been joined here with great intensity and the rebels won it hands down.

The town of Zawia rose against Gaddafi and its proximity to Tripoli was important. There were conflicting reports in the media, but the Gaddafi regime claimed to be in control there, though much depends on how we interpret this claim.

An early rebellion by the Berbers in the Gebel Nefusa towards the Tunisian border is significant. The Berbers have long been suppressed by the Gaddafi regime and had been unable to garner international support for their cause. The wider Berber community may become more involved in the Libyan problem, if this uprising is successful.[4]

Gaddafi had been in power for forty-two years, since September 1969, and had made many enemies. He had culled a number of them but not all. How secure was he against a home-grown coup or an attempt by the West to bring about regime change? Libya had become a police state and the security services were akin to the East German Stasi, on which they were modelled. The intelligence services were carefully controlled and vertically segregated; that is, they did not communicate with each other and reported upwards to a central co-ordinating group situated within Gaddafi's protected compound at Bab Azzizia in Tripoli.

There are some points to note here, too. The first is that Gaddafi had gathered the reins of power into his own hands and those of his family and tribe. Observers have called this the re-tribalisation of Libya. The second is that the real wielders of power were to be found in the state security system, which is notably opaque, even to foreign diplomats whose job it is to identify such people. In the *Guardian* of 31 March 2011, Peter Beaumont makes this point by quoting Sir Richard Dalton, a former British ambassador to Libya. Dalton reportedly said:

> [Gaddafi's] sons see themselves as heirs, modelled on Gulf princes. Without any concrete roles they get things done by getting on the telephone and making it happen. It is about patronage … [The security service] is totally and utterly opaque. So much so it is incredibly difficult to interpret the lines of command. Then there is this mysterious entity called the old guard. In the end I tried to avoid using it because it was so hard to say who they were … So long as the internal security is still intact and still taking orders, the regime in Tripoli can survive.

Gaddafi was personally protected by a praetorian guard and his sons and daughter formed an inner Cabinet which was to become more powerful as the rebellion continued. The crack army unit, used for the suppression of demonstrations, was commanded by Kamis, Muammar Gaddafi's son and one of the closest associates.

How did matters stand for Gaddafi in West Libya on the brink of the uprising in Benghazi? I argue that the tribal nature of Libya is crucial. In Tripolitania the Warfella, the Wana Farash and the Tarhunis tribes have considerable influence. Gaddafi appears to have dispatched army units to the Warfella tribe's traditional homeland of Beni Walid to make sure that it did not join the uprising in Misurata and Zawia.

Writing in the *New York Times* on 14 March 2011, David Kirkpatrick stated that he had received an anonymous note from a Warfella tribal leader who wrote: '... The Warfalla [sic], like their brethren the Zintan and Awlad Suleiman are boiling. The only reason we have not seen them participate in combat is the lack of weapons, and the siege that is now implemented upon them. They are simply outgunned, and are vulnerable.'

There was clearly some uncertainty. Ian Black, writing for the *Guardian* from Beni Walid on 23 March, said:

> No significant Warfalla [sic] figure is involved in the opposition despite early claims that the entire tribe had defected. There has been talk of large cash payments to ensure they did not – or changed sides again. According to rumours in Tripoli, key tribes have been offered large sums of money to ensure that they toe the line at this time of unprecedented danger to the regime. Tribal leaders can be seen in their finery in the capital's best hotel and being driven around in the sleek government vehicles reserved for VIPs.

The battle for the support of the major tribes opened quickly.

For all his calculations, Gaddafi ran out of time to crush the Benghazi rebellion. The French and British governments had been working hard to construct a consensus in favour of military intervention on the good and clear evidence that Gaddafi was murdering civilians. President Sarkozy of France was taking the lead, perhaps to boost his popularity ratings which had slipped alarmingly. The Arab League was in favour of intervention since a number of its members were less than happy with Gaddafi, though their contribution was unlikely to extend further than diplomatic manoeuvring.

The USA was wary. The CIA had been concerned for some time about the uncomfortable presence of Libyan jihadists in Derna and Benghazi, who had been involved in the Afghan war. Libya watchers, and there must have been some in the CIA, MI6 and elsewhere, will not have forgotten the Islamic fundamentalist violence in the Gebel Akhdar of Cyrenaica – now called East Libya – between 1995 and 1998. The violence was fomented and largely controlled by the Libyan Islamic Fighting Group. It was ruthlessly suppressed by Gaddafi using the Libyan air force, though the aircraft that did the strafing and bombing were flown by Cubans and Serbs.

There was also a lingering sensitivity about a discredited source of intelligence concerning weapons of mass destruction in Iraq, which had deliberately misled and subsequently embarrassed both Tony Blair and George Bush.

Angela Merkel, the German Chancellor, was notably reluctant to support intervention and in France Sarkozy was not on the best of terms with his Foreign Secretary. The British prime minister, David Cameron, was furiously committed to intervention. He was fortunate because his coalition partners in government were of like mind and the pressure from non-interventionists was thus reduced. He was hamstrung because he and his government had decommissioned an aircraft carrier and its complement of Harrier jets, which would have been the best option for deployment in the event of a No Fly Zone being imposed over Libya.

At first, no one was too sure how safe it was to support the 17 February rebels. Had the Libyan Islamic Fighting Group re-emerged? A number of them were recently released from Abu Salim jail and they may have been keeping a low profile whilst organising and arming to emerge at an opportune moment. The gates of the army barracks in Benghazi had been breached by a suicide bomber and they are not easily found and launched at a target.

Were there signs of stable, strong and mature leadership? It was essential to look the leaders in the eye and test their resolve. The British sent an MI6 mission from their temporary special forces base in Malta. For six months MI6 had a man in place in Benghazi. He worked as an administrator with a company, some miles out of town. He had been in contact with anti-Gaddafi people who were, apparently, ready to meet a British mission.

The two MI6 men, with a six-man SAS escort, landed near an agreed rendezvous in their helicopter and set off to find their contact, only to be met by a group of armed and militant farmers who thought they were the enemy. They were taken into custody and it took time to get them released and dispatched to the docks in Benghazi to go home with British evacuees.

The French did it differently. The scene was set for a drama, which was characteristic of both France and Libya. As the residents of Benghazi took stock of their situation, a number of lawyers and professionals set up a provisional council in the law courts, over which they raised the flag of the old Kingdom of Libya. It took time and courage. Benghazi has long culti-vated a tradition of heated debate.

On Saturday 5 March, the Libyan opposition movement nominated an Interim National Transition Council to lay the foundations for a government. Not all the members were named for security reasons.

The first council had thirty-two members representing various regions and cities. Mustafa Abdul Jalil was elected chairman. A judge from Baida, he was Justice Minister under Gaddafi but resigned after the uprising began. As chairman of the council, he had a price on his head believed to be 500,000 Libyan dinars.

Mohammed Jebril, the former Gaddafi government man with a PhD from the University of Pittsburgh, and Ali Aziz el Esawi, the former Libyan ambassador to India and a sometime minister for the economy, trade and investment, were made responsible for foreign affairs.

Abdul Hafiz Ghoga, head of the Benghazi lawyers syndi-cate, was appointed vice-chairman and spokesman. Other lawyers on the council were Dr Abdulla Moussa al Mayhoub, sometime dean of the law faculty of Gar Yunis University, Benghazi; Fathi Turbil, the human rights lawyer; and Dr Salwa Fawzi el Deghali, who taught in the Academy of Graduate Studies in Benghazi, was made head the legal advisory com-mittee. Ahmed al Abbar, whose ancestors were prominent in the guerrilla war during the late Italian occupation, held the economics brief. Omar Hariri, the military member of the council, is said to have been one of Gaddafi's conspirators in the 1969 coup, but was later jailed by the regime.

A military council of fifteen, including Omar Hariri, was also set up. The most interesting figure appears to be Staff General Abdul Fatah Yunis, who had resigned as Gaddafi's Interior Minister on 20 February. Yunis was also with Gaddafi in the 1969 coup.[5] Later, in protest over the Gaddafi brutal-ity, Kailifa Huftar, a native of Benghazi who was a retired Libyan general, also joined the Military Council. He became the general commanding the rebel forces. Early disagreements amongst members of the Military Council led to disquiet and

Italy, France and Britain later sent teams of military advisors to get the staff work sorted out.

When Benghazi was in peril the Interim National Council needed outside help. One of France's controversial and colourful personalities arrived in a greengrocer's van to rescue them. The romance, for that it certainly was, has gained credence in Benghazi and may become the accepted version of events.

Bernard-Henry Lévy was the hero. He has been described as an 'inescapable figure of mockery, amusement, and envy in his native France … a man of inherited wealth … a socialist whose trademarks – flowing hair, black suits, unbuttoned white shirts, thin blond women – can undercut his passionate campaigning on public causes'.[6]

Lévy, or BHL as he is known in France, was a friend of Nicholas Sarkozy. The friendship was complicated by differing political views and by a connection with Carla Bruni, the current Mrs Sarkozy, who had a child by BHL's sometime son-in-law.

The story may be challenged in detail, but it is corroborated by a number of sources.[7] Lévy had been in Egypt to cover the events following the Arab Spring uprising. He got wind of events in Libya but was called back to Paris on business. On 27 February he contacted President Sarkozy and suggested that he was travelling to Benghazi and might contact the rebels. He appears to have obtained Sarkozy's blessing, though what passed between them is unlikely to emerge. Lévy suggests, and he is probably right, that Sarkozy was looking for a way to contact the rebels but had no idea who to talk to.

Lévy chartered an aircraft and flew to Mersah Matruh, the nearest Egyptian airport to Sollum on the Libyan border. He was accompanied by Gilles Hertzog and the photographer Marc Rousell. They found the border crowded with refugees but managed to gain entry to Libya early on 1 March. They found a van loaded with vegetables on its way to Tobruk, in which they bought or begged a ride. From Tobruk they went to Baida and were said to have met the chairman of the Transitional Council, with whom they travelled to Benghazi.

Lévy, Hertzog and Rousell reached the Tebesti Hotel in Benghazi, where they heard that there was to be a meeting in a private villa of the National Transition Council on 3 March. Lévy, who implied that he was the personal representative of the French president, managed to insinuate himself into the meeting. This was, perhaps, his finest moment.

Lévy addressed the meeting with a short speech and then asked if he might contact President Sarkozy. There was nothing to lose and the council agreed. Apparently using an old cell phone, he contacted President Sarkozy personally. On 5 March, Sarkozy issued a press release, in which he welcomed the formation of the Interim National Council. This was the council's first sign of legitimacy. The news brought hope and a number of French flags sprouted around Benghazi.

By the following Monday, Lévy was in Paris and in contact with President Sarkozy. By Thursday, National Transition councillor Mohammed Jebril was in Sarkozy's office in the Elysee Palace and an agreement of considerable importance was reached. Sarkozy agreed to recognise the National Transitional Council as the legitimate government of Libya. Lévy, who was present, implied that the council was certainly not asking for troops on the ground but for the imposition of a No Fly Zone. Sarkozy agreed to bomb three key airfields in Libya, notably the one in the south used for receiving mercenaries from Chad and elsewhere.

The diplomatic agreement was announced by Sarkozy without the knowledge of the French Foreign Minister, who heard it when getting off a train in Brussels on his way to a conference. David Cameron had, however, been forewarned.

Sarkozy now needed a UN Security Council resolution in favour of intervention. For this he needed the USA to approve. He believed he had the UK on his side and he could persuade the EU, the Arab League and the African Union.

Good fortune played another card: Hilary Clinton was due in Paris for a G8 meeting on 14 March. She agreed to meet Jebril then. He travelled to Paris on that day and was met by Lévy at Le Bourget.

Jebril found his meeting disappointing and was very upset. He was sure he had failed to convince Mrs Clinton. He had a nervous and depressing wait in Lévy's apartment until 4 p.m., when Sarkozy called to say that the USA was minded to cast a vote in the UN in favour of intervention.

On Thursday 17 March, resolution 1973 was put before the UN Security Council in New York, where France, Britain and the USA were among the ten who voted in favour of the use of all necessary means to protect civilian lives in Libya. Russia and China were among the five nations that abstained.

On 19 March, Tomahawk missiles fired from US and UK navy vessels hit air defences around Tripoli and Misurata, and French jets attacked Gaddafi's armoury near Benghazi. The city was saved but just in time. Tanks were in its western approaches and Gaddafi's snipers were firing from buildings very close to the rebel headquarters in the courthouse.

It would be as well to remember that President Obama, for a number of reasons no doubt, offered crucial but limited assistance and required NATO to assume command of the No Fly Zone.

A headline in *The Times* of London dated 26 July 2011 was remarkably imperialistic. It stated: 'Britain will let Gaddafi stay – if he steps down.' Somehow Muammar Gaddafi continued to hold out in Tripoli for several months, despite the huge effort NATO had made to end his regime.

The military expenditure for the NATO countries had been high. The sophisticated military hardware and software of the early twenty-first century had been lavishly deployed against him. Battle management aircraft, such as AWACS and surveillance drones, had been used. Missiles with pinpoint accuracy and Apache helicopters had been launched from NATO ships offshore. Military advisors had been sent to help the anti-Gaddafi forces. Diplomacy and rhetoric had been ratcheted up to isolate his regime. Threats of prosecution for war crimes had been made to encourage Gaddafi's close supporters to defect. President Zuma of South Africa had visited him to negotiate a settlement. Sanctions had been applied and an oil pipeline cut to starve Tripoli of fuel. In spite of all this, he had clung on.

The NATO powers were not prepared for a long campaign. British military chiefs were warning that they could not sustain their Libyan commitments as well as those in Afghanistan. For the British prime minister the Conservative Party conference was looming and he did not want the Libyan problem to unsettle his supporters. President Obama was focusing on re-election. It had to end. How it did and what happened afterwards is for others to write about.

Not the first Libyan ruler to withstand the might of the USA, Gaddafi survived for so long for a number of reasons. One of these reasons is to be found in his personality, one in the history of Libya and one in the constraints upon NATO which limited its intervention, not to mention the fact that Gaddafi had access to weaponry and mercenaries.

Which Way Now For Libya?

The Arab Spring of 2011 brought protesters to the streets of Cairo. Protesters in Benghazi appeared to be emulating them but with a difference. There is oil and gas below the surface of Libya and Gaddafi was a different character to Hosni Mubarak. He was not short of supporters. His family and tribe were not about to go quietly.

The problems faced by modern rulers of Libya are manifold. The ambitions of the people of Benghazi differ from those of the Misuratans. The Berbers of the Gebel Nefusa need to be free to express their culture and the problems of the Tebu and the Tuareg in the Fezzan will not be easy solved. There is also the connection with radical Islam which needs to be sorted out otherwise it will alarm the West.

Tripoli has always been a city state and its inhabitants have for so long perceived themselves as superior. How to integrate it into a greater Libya will be a challenge. So will the awful urge to take revenge on Gaddafi loyalists. A killing spree would alienate the world.

Support for the National Transition Council had been shaken by the killing of the rebel army commander General Yunis, which was announced on Friday 29 July 2011. He had been Gaddafi's Minister of the Interior before defecting to the rebels. He was an ambitious man and there may have been blood on his hands and human rights violations to account for. He had enemies amongst the rebels for certain. That there are a number of armed factions with their own agendas to peruse is disconcerting. The killing on 28 July 2011 of General Abdul Fatah Yunis by a rebel group with an Islamist agenda shows how difficult it will be to reconcile the warring groups peacefully. It also suggests that the military strongmen have the means to seize power.

Spending the oil revenues with enlightenment will not be easy. Somehow the people of Libya must learn not to rely on migrant workers to do their laundry and bake their bread. There is no room for modern slavery. The problems of great wealth are not easy to solve.

The Egyptian experiment with democracy will be watched closely in Libya and the reaction of her neighbours to the south, such as Chad, Burkina Faso and Niger, will prove interesting. Some are ruled by Gaddafi's friends and have benefited from his largess. They have supplied mercenaries for his armies and made treaties which will embarrass a new Libyan government.

Britain, the USA and France have intervened and will not be able to shirk their responsibilities. Libya is not remote like Afghanistan; it is perilously near Italy and Greece, both of which are insecure politically and economically.

Afterword

The summary execution of Muammar Gaddafi in Sirte on 20 October 2011 has brought to an end a disturbing period in Libya's history. His capture as his convoy attempted an escape was accomplished with the aid of an air strike by NATO. Clearly a sophisticated system of target identification, command and control was developed by NATO, which is likely to be a model for other such interventions in the future. The story of the military co-operation between the anti-Gaddafi militias and NATO will no doubt emerge soon.

The image of the dead dictator was spread instantly and widely by means of mobile phone images. Indeed the power of personal communications has escaped the control of even the most dominant of despots and will shape the democratic process in ways we have yet to understand. Mobile phones, Facebook and Twitter played a crucial part in the Arab Spring and will help to undermine other dictatorial regimes in the future.

That Muammar Gaddafi and members of his close family and entourage were swiftly executed will cause some problems. The nature of the Libyan secret services made him and his close family the repository of much valuable information. His astounding self-delusion, which has been discussed at some length in this book, will exercise the minds of historians and psychologists for some time to come.

For the second time the Libyan people have fought for their freedom, but this time they have won. Will they lose it again through infighting and internal discord? They will certainly be watched with interest and some anxiety as they shape their future. Gaddafi's legacy may still be malignant; hours after his death there were reports of tribal differences, which must trouble the new government as it attempts to assert control.

The vast quantity of oil and natural gas below the Libyan Desert and the Gulf of Sirte gives the Libyans the potential to lead their brothers and sisters in Egypt, Tunisia and Syria in making the Arab Spring into a democratic summer. On the other hand, their history and internal divisions may cause considerable unrest. The country is awash with arms and there is no democratic tradition to help the people establish a parliamentary system and a strong and responsive government.

The Interim National Council was formed by lawyers to give some leadership to the 17 February uprising in Benghazi. It vowed to disband as soon as the battle for Libya was over and the democratic process was set in train. But any semblance of democracy must be preceded by reconciliation, and to forgive and forget the enmities that have arisen in the civil war will not be easy. It was achieved for a while in South Africa but there is no Nelson Mandela or Desmond Tutu in Libya. There are, however, rival tribal and militia leaders who will want their contribution to the downfall of Gaddafi recognised by any future government.

The British and French invested much political capital and not a little treasure in the outcome, though both were restrained by their old colonial legacies and chastened by the mistakes made during the disastrous occupation of Iraq. It is not difficult, even now, to accuse them of imperialism should they interfere too overtly in Libyan affairs. However, they cannot afford for Libya to fall into the hands of militant Islamists, or for it to become a Somalia on the Mediterranean shore. The Egyptians, who look with anxiety at their unruly neighbour, also have an interest in a stable outcome. Their military is likely to be on the *qui vive* but wary of intervention; there has always been a love-hate relationship between the two countries. These powerful off-stage players may give strength to the new Libyan government, while the prospect of a more equitable distribution of the oil wealth may restrain the hotheads and the maligned.

The sparsely populated south of Libya, the old province of the Fezzan, has not yet been won over by the National

Transition Council. This area is contiguous with countries which were not unfriendly to the Gaddafi regime and the reaction of Niger, Chad, Burkina Faso and the Sudan will be interesting. A number of Gaddafi's mercenaries were recruited from these countries and their treatment by the revolutionary militias will be of some consequence.

China has been making a belated effort to achieve a rapport with the Interim National Council because it has a ferocious appetite for oil. Reports from Benghazi of efforts by foreign oil companies to steal a march on their rivals have been disconcerting. The oil fields will need expertise and investment to bring them back into production and to find and exploit new reserves. We must hope that the new Libyan government will be honest and above board in its dealings with the oil companies, who are at best pragmatic and at worst unscrupulous.

There is still a great deal of sophisticated military hardware at large. The command and control systems have been heavily damaged and some of the big assets neutralised. However, while the expenditure on armaments was notably high under Gaddafi, much of the equipment was too difficult to maintain and operate. Similarly, the Libyan air force was lavishly equipped but grounded during the civil war. The country will need defending in the future and it will be difficult to steer an ethical course through the rivalries in the global armament business. It will certainly try hard to exploit a new market for its lethal wares.

There is a final, major challenge which has been too often overlooked. The population of Libya has been growing apace and the percentage of young people is very high indeed. Unless they are given a stake in their country's future and given real work to do there will be trouble. The role of women in the new Libya will also be crucial and watched with interest throughout the Muslim world.

Sadly, Gaddafi's legacy to Libya will be found in the graves of his many victims and of those who gave their lives to wrest a semblance of freedom from his rule.

John Oakes
20 October 2011
Libyastories.com

Notes

1 The Greeks, the Romans and the Garamantes

1 Julian Thompson and the Imperial War Museum, *The Imperial War Museum Book of War Behind Enemy Lines*, Sidgwick & Jackson (in association with the Imperial War Museum), London and Basingstoke, 1998.

2 Seaton Dearden (ed.), *Tulley's Ten Years of Residence at the Court of Tripoli*, Limited Edition, Arthur Barker, London, 1957, p. 204.

3 More can be learnt about this intriguing civilisation by reading *The Archaeology of the Fezzan*, published in 2003 by the Society of Libyan Studies, London and the Department of Antiquities, Tripoli.

4 Geoffrey Rickman, *The Corn Supply of Ancient Rome*, Clarendon Press, Oxford, 1980, p. 197.

5 E. W. Bovill, *The Golden Trade of the Moors*, Oxford University Press, London, 1963, pp. 33, 37–8.

6 Ibid., pp. 22–39.

7 A.R. Burns, *The Pelican History of Greece*, Penguin Books, London, 1974, p. 96.

2 The Arab Invasion: The True Bedouin Arrive

1 W.C. Smith, *Islam in Modern History*, Princeton University Press, 1957, p. 95.

2 One notable upheaval occurred in 1832 in the eastern region called the Barqua. The tribes that now occupy this region drove out a number of tribes, which now range the littoral of the western Sirtica. These displaced tribes are known as al Arab al Gharb, the western Arabs.

3 E.E. Evans-Pritchard, *The Sanusi of Cyrenaica*, Oxford University Press, 1973, pp. 46–7.

4 E. W. Bovill, *The Golden Trade of the Moors*, Oxford University Press, London, 1963, pp. 58–9.

3 Ottomans and Turks: The Slave Trade, the Barbary Corsairs and the Four-Year War with the USA

1 Hugh Thomas, *The Slave Trade, The History of the Atlantic Slave Trade 1440–1870*, Picador, London, 1997, p. 561.
2 Douglas Porch, *The Conquest of the Sahara*, Oxford University Press, 1984, pp. 58–60.
3 John Wright, *A History of Libya*, Hurst and Company, London, 1988, p. 95.
4 The Karamanli family was still in Tripoli in 1958 and I have a strong recollection of meeting Mr Karamanli.
5 Seaton Dearden (ed.), *Tulley's Ten Years of Residence at the Court of Tripoli*, Limited Edition, Arthur Barker, London, 1957, p 71. Note original spelling has been retained.
6 *Slavery in Africa*, Microsoft Encarta Online Encyclopaedia, 2000, http:// encarta.msn.com.
7 Seaton Dearden, *A Nest of Coursairs, The Fighting Karamanlis of the Barbary Coast*, John Murray, London, 1976, pp. 156–201.
8 E.E. Evans-Pritchard, *The Sanusi of Cyrenaica*, Oxford University Press, 1973, p. 144.

4 Italian Libya: The Battle for the Sword of Islam

1 Andrew Mango, *Attatürk*, John Murray, London, 1999, pp. 101–11.
2 *La pacifaction della Cireniaca*, Revista delle Colonie Italiane, 1932, p. 64.
3 E.E. Evans-Pritchard, *The Sanusi of Cyrenaica*, Oxford University Press, 1973, p. 165.
4 Dates from Ibid., p. 174.
5 Emrys L. Peters, *The Bedouin of Cyrenaica*, Jack Goody and Emanuel Marx (eds), Cambridge University Press, 1990, p. 30.
6 E.E. Evans-Pritchard, *The Sanusi of Cyrenaica*, Oxford University Press, 1973, pp. 162–3.
7 John Wright, *A History of Libya*, Hurst and Company, London, 2010, p. 150.
8 K. Holmboe, *Desert Encounter, An Adventurous Journey through Italian Africa*, London, 1936, p. 207. Quoted in John Wright, *A History of Libya*, Hurst and Company, London, 2010, pp. 148–9.

5 Second World War in Libya: The Desert Rats, the Desert Fox and the Free French

1 John Connell, *Wavell*, Harcourt Brace & Ward, New York, 1956, p. 262.
2 A number of Tripolitanian sheikhs dissociated themselves from the decision, intending, it was said, to make a separate offer.
3 In 1965, a commander in the Libyan Customs Service from Derna visited me in my office in Benghazi. I asked if he had known of Popski for he was old enough to have done so, having lived in Derna during the war. He said that he did and recounted some of the stories Popski told in his book.

Whilst he may have read the book, which is unlikely, his stories, nevertheless, had a ring of truth.

4 Julian Thompson, *The Imperial War Museum Book of War Behind Enemy Lines*,
   Sidgwick & Jackson, London, 1998, p. 41.

5 *L'histoire en 1,000 images. La Guerre 1939–1945*, Circle Europée du Livre, Paris,
   1963, p. 79.

6 Paraphrased from Jay A. Stout, *Fortress Ploesti, The Campaign to Destroy Hitler's
   Oil*, Casemate, Havertown, PA, 2003.

7 www.ladybegood.com.

6 Independence: A Child of the United Nations

1 Quoted in a 'Letter from Libya', Joseph Wechsberg, *New Yorker*, 10 November
   1951.

7 The Kingdom of Libya: The Shepherd King and the Oil Barons

1 Julian Thompson and the Imperial War Museum, *The Imperial War Museum
   Book of War Behind Enemy Lines*, Sidgwick & Jackson (in association with the
   Imperial War Museum), London and Basingstoke, 1998, p. 34.

2 Francis Williams, *A Prime Minister Remembers*, Heinemann, London, 1961, p. 178.

3 Dirk Vandewalle, *A History of Libya*, Cambridge University Press, 2006, p. 45.

4 Edward J. Epstein, *Dossier, The Secret History of Armand Hammer*, Orion
   Business Books, London, 1998, p. 217. Epstein's source for this assertion
   is the testimony of James Akins before the US Senate Foreign Relations
   Committee on 11 October 1973.

5 *Time*, 9 April 1956.

6 Peter Townsend, *Bactria and Zoraster*, Privately Published, Reading, 2007, p. 28.

7 Vanderwalle, p. 65.

8 Ibid., p. 59.

9 Edward J. Epstein, *Dossier, The Secret History of Armand Hammer*, Orion
   Business Books, London, 1998.

10 David Blundy and Andrew Lycett, *Qaddafi and the Libya Revolution*, Corgi
    Books, London, 1988, p. 66.

11 From the letter of abdication of King Idris dated 4 August 1969: 'Most men's
    work is not completely devoid of imperfections, and when some years ago
    I felt weak. I offered my resignation, but you returned it. I obeyed your wish
    and withdrew it. Now, due to my advanced years and weak body I find
    myself obliged to say for the second time that I am unable to carry this
    heavy responsibility.'

8 Gaddafi I: Companions of the Tent

1 Muammar Gaddafi and Edmond Jouve, *My Vision*, John Blake, London, 2005, p. 154.
2 Ibid., pp. 81–2.
3 Ronald Bruce St John, *Libya, From Colony to Independence*, Oneworld, Oxford, 2008, pp. 135–6.
4 Peter Mansfield, *The Arabs*, Penguin Books, London, 1980, p. 539. This certainly applied to the Libyans.
5 Emrys Peters is the acknowledged authority on the Bedouin tribes of Cyrenaica. For further amplification see: Emrys L. Peters, *The Bedouin of Cyrenaica*, Jack Goody and Emanuel Marx (eds), Cambridge University Press, 1990.
6 Ronald Bruce St John, *Libya, From Colony to Independence*, Oneworld, Oxford, 2008, pp. 141–2.
7 Arnold Toynbee's introduction to Sami Hadawwi, *Palestine Diary*, Volume 1, Beirut, 1969, pp. xii–xiv.
8 Muammar Gaddafi and Edmond Jouve, *My Vision*, John Blake, London, 2005, p. 82.
9 David Blundy and Andrew Lycett, *Qaddafi and the Libya Revolution*, Corgi Books, London, 1988, pp. 58–60.
10 Dirk Vandewalle, *A History of Libya*, Cambridge University Press, 2006, p. 81.
11 There was a US army military mission in Benghazi and the logistics specialist was my neighbour for some time.

9 Gaddafi II: The Pariah State and Human Rights Issues

1 Ronald Bruce St John, *Libya, From Colony to Independence*, Oneworld, Oxford, 2008, pp. 140–1.
2 Denis Healy, *The Time of My Life*, Michael Joseph, London, 1989, p. 322.
3 JoeProBono, http://www.freerepublic.com/focus/f-bloggers/2680460/posts, retrieved 25 June 2011.
4 Edward J. Epstein, *Dossier, The Secret History of Armand Hammer*, Orion Business Books, London, 1998, pp. 240–5.
5 M. Al Gathafi, *The Green Book – The Solution to the Problem of Democracy: The Solution to Economic Problems; The Social Basis of the Third Universal Theory*, Ithaca Press, Reading, 2005, p. 27.
6 Ronald Bruce St John, *Libya, From Colony to Independence*, Oneworld, Oxford, 2008, pp. 169–71.
7 The Human Rights Watch, www.hrw.org, report dated 27 June 2006.
8 Alison Pargeter, *Terrorism Monitor*, Volume 3, Issue 5, www.jamestown.org.

10   Gaddafi III: Weapons of Mass Destruction, the IRA, St James's Square and Lockerbie

1   The data is summarised from *The Libyan Military Guide*, accessed from globalsecurity.com; Hanspeter Mattes, *Challenges of Security Governance in the Middle East*, accessed free online; The Libyan Case, 2004 from 'Soldiers to Policemen: Quadhafi's Army in the New Century' by Paola De Maio, first published in the *Journal of Middle Eastern Politics* and accessed free online.

2   Alasdair McKay, *The Janjaweed in Darfur; Echoes of Gaddafi's Islamic Legion*, www.defenceviewpoints.co.uk.

3   All weapons of mass destruction data from the CRS report 'Disarming Libya: Weapons of Mass Destruction', by Sahron A. Squassoni and Andrew Feickert, April 2004, Congressional Research Service, US Library of Congress, Order Code RS21823. Additional information from www.globalsecurity.org.

4   Gaddafi's role in arming the IRA has been well covered in: Brendan O'Brien, *The Long War: the IRA and Sinn Féin, from Armed Struggle to Peace Talks* and E. Maloney, *A Secret History of The IRA*, Penguin, London, 2007.

5   fenian32.blogspot.com.

6   David Blundy and Andrew Lycett, *Quaddafi and the Libyan Revolution*, Corgi, London, 1988, p. 95.

7   A detailed account of these shipments is in Toby Harnden's book, *Bandit Country: the IRA and South Armagh*, Hodder & Stoughton, 1999.

8   David Blundy and Andrew Lycett, *Quaddafi and the Libyan Revolution*, Corgi, London, 1988, p. 187.

9   Ibid., p. 191.

10   Ian Black, *Guardian*, 8 July 1999.

11   *Guardian*, Wednesday 23 July 1997.

12   Sources: BBC, *The Times*, *Guardian*, 17 February.

13   Data taken from the Aviation Safety Network at www.flightsafety.org.

11   Challenging Muammar Gaddafi

1   The Libyan government has not published figures about military expenditure for a number of years. These figures are similar to those found on www.globalsecurity.com and published by *The Times* and other newspapers. Providing all these weapons were serviceable, which they will certainly not have been, and all the troops remained loyal, which they did not, the rebels would have faced considerable opposition. There are the police to take into account; strangely so, because Gaddafi once abolished them, so we must assume that they were pseudo-policemen.

2   Sources: *The Times*, *Telegraph*, *New York Times*, *Guardian*, *Time*, *Newsweek*.

3   *The Times*, 22 February 2011.

4   www.hrw.org.

5   He was killed by a rebel group on 28 July 2011.

6   Steven Erlanger, http://www.newyorker.com/online/blogs/movies/2011/03/bernard-henri-levy-nato-libya.html.

7   *New York Times*, *Huffington Post*, *Time* and *Newsweek*.

Select Bibliography

Blundy, David and Lycett, Andrew, *Qaddafi and the Libya Revolution*, Corgi Books, London, 1988.

Bovill, E.W., *The Golden Trade of the Moors*, Oxford University Press, London, 1963.

Burns, A.R., *The Pelican History of Greece*, Penguin Books, London, 1974.

Connell, John, *Wavell, Harcourt Brace & Ward*, New York, 1956.

Dearden, Seaton, *A Nest of Coursairs, the Fighting Karamanlis of the Barabary Coast*, John Murray, London, 1976.

—————— (ed.), *Tulley's Ten Years of Residence at the Court of Tripoli*, Limited Edition, Arthur Barker, London, 1957.

Epstein, Edward J., *Dossier, the Secret History of Armand Hammer*, Orion Business Books, London, 1998.

Evans-Pritchard, E.E., *The Sanusi of Cyrenaica*, Oxford University Press, 1973.

Gaddafi, Muammar and Jouve, Edmond, *My Vision*, John Blake, London, 2005.

Gathafi, M.Al, *The Green Book – the Solution to the Problem of Democracy: the Solution to Economic Problems; the Social Basis of the Third Universal Theory*, Ithaca Press, Reading, 2005.

Harnden, Toby, *Bandit Country: the IRA and South Armagh*, Hodder & Stoughton, London, 1999.

Healy, Denis, *The Time of My Life*, Michael Joseph, London, 1989.

Maloney, E., *A Secret History of the IRA*, Penguin, London, 2007.

Mango, Andrew, *Attatürk*, John Murray, London, 1999.

Mansfield, Peter, *The Arabs*, Penguin Books, London, 1980.

O'Brein, Brendon, *The Long War, the IRA and Sinn Féin, from Armed Struggle to Peace Talks*.

Peters, Emrys L., *The Bedouin of Cyrenaica*, Jack Goody and Emanuel Marx (eds), Cambridge University Press, 1990.

Porch, Douglas, *The Conquest of the Sahara*, Oxford University Press, London, 1984.

Rickman, Geoffrey, *The Corn Supply of Ancient Rome*, Clarendon Press, Oxford, 1980.

Smith, W.C., *Islam in Modern History*, Princeton University Press, 1957.

St John, Ronald Bruce, *Libya, From Colony to Independence*, Oneworld, Oxford, 2008.

Stout, Jay A., *Fortress Ploesti: The Campaign to Destroy Hitler's Oil*, Casemate, Havertown, PA, 2003.

Thomas, Hugh, *The Slave Trade, the History of the Atlantic Slave Trade 1440–1870*, Picador, London, 1997.

Thompson, Julian and the Imperial War Museum, *The Imperial War Museum Book of War Behind Enemy Lines*, Sidgwick & Jackson (in association with the Imperial War Museum), London and Basingstoke, 1998.

Townsend, Peter, *Bactria and Zoraster*, Privately Published, Reading, 2007.

Vandewalle, Dirk, *A History of Libya*, Cambridge Univeristy Press, 2006.

Williams, Francis, *A Prime Minister Remembers*, Heinemann, London, 1961.

Wright, John, *A History of Libya*, Hurst and Company, London, 1988.

Index

Visit our website and discover thousands of other History Press books.

www.thehistorypress.co.uk